From *The Freshman* (1925): life can be like the movies.

AN
AMERICAN
COMEDY

by

HAROLD LLOYD

written in collaboration with
WESLEY W. STOUT

with an Introductory Note by
RICHARD GRIFFITH

and the text of a 1966 Harold Lloyd interview:
"The Serious Business of Being Funny," conducted and edited by
HUBERT I. COHEN
ASSISTANT PROFESSOR (AMERICAN LITERATURE AND FILM),
DEPARTMENT OF HUMANITIES, COLLEGE OF ENGINEERING,
UNIVERSITY OF MICHIGAN

DOVER PUBLICATIONS, INC.

NEW YORK

Published in Canada by General Publishing Company, Ltd., 30 Lesmill Road, Don Mills, Toronto, Ontario.
Published in the United Kingdom by Constable and Company, Ltd., 10 Orange Street, London WC 2.

This Dover edition, first published in 1971, is an unabridged republication, with minor corrections, of the work originally published in 1928 by Longmans, Green & Co., New York, with the title *An American Comedy: Acted by Harold Lloyd, Directed by Wesley W. Stout*. The present edition is published by special arrangement with Harold Lloyd.

The present edition includes the following new features:

(1) A selection of 37 additional pictures.

(2) A new Index.

(3) A new Introductory Note by Richard Griffith.

(4) An Appendix containing the text of an interview with Harold Lloyd, "The Serious Business of Being Funny," conducted and edited by Hubert I. Cohen. This interview (Copyright © 1969 by Film Comment Publishing Corporation) was originally published, in a somewhat different form, in Volume 5, Number 3 (Fall 1969 issue) of *Film Comment*, and is reprinted here by the kind permission of Austin F. Lamont, Managing Editor of *Film Comment*, and of Hubert I. Cohen.

International Standard Book Number: 0-486-22684-0
Library of Congress Catalog Card Number: 70-133257

Manufactured in the United States of America
Dover Publications, Inc.
180 Varick Street
New York, N.Y. 10014

Introductory Note

BY

RICHARD GRIFFITH*

THIS IS Lloyd's only autobiography, and no other biography exists.† It seems incredible, especially in this day when so much is being published about the movies.

The lack of a definitive late book on Lloyd reflects the disesteem in which he has traditionally been held by the movie highbrows. They do not like his optimism. His calculated comedy methods have been labeled "mechanical" and let go at that. His wealth and success have naturally been held against him. But it's the optimism which chiefly sticks in the highbrow craw and accounts for the continued fundamental lack of interest in him and the continued rating of him below Chaplin, Keaton and even Langdon. *Weltschmerz* is hard to find in him, and *Weltschmerz* is of course essential.

This is largely nonsense. The "boy with the glasses" character is as full of significance as Keaton's frozen man from Mars, and of greater significance than Langdon's old baby. To a Lloyd, life's perils are to be overcome, but they are real perils none the less and by no means entirely "exterior," as alleged. What is probably his masterpiece, *Grandma's Boy,* is full of both peril and horror, decidedly interior.

*This is a slightly abridged and edited version of a written note Mr. Griffith prepared for Dover Publications in June 1969. His death occurred before he could write a full introduction to the Dover edition of *An American Comedy;* this brief but incisive statement must stand in the place of that introduction.—THE PUBLISHER.

†The autobiographical articles in *Photoplay,* May–July 1924 and December 1925, are earlier than the present book. The brief biographical sections in William Cahn's book *Harold Lloyd's World of Comedy* (Duell, Sloan and Pearce, N. Y., 1964) take the story into the sixties, but are only outlines of a biography.—THE PUBLISHER.

Scene from *Mad Wednesday*, by Preston Sturges, with Harold Lloyd, Jimmy Conlin and Jackie the lion. A further twist in the danger-on-the-window-ledge motif.

Be that as it may, this is a valuable book for the film scholar and for anyone who truly loves the film medium per se. Lloyd's account of his early struggles underlines and fleshes out the emerging fact that basic film comedy technique was invented *just before* films became the dominant form of entertainment— invented by those self-taught men of the theatrical underworld who entertained uneducated people with whom they were in everyday close contact. What they invented, in their vaudevilles, circuses, "stock companies" and tent shows, owed a minimum to theatrical tradition and a maximum to their knowledge of their audiences; they mostly thought it all up themselves as they went along. To such men, and they included Sennett, Chaplin, Keaton, Langdon and Arbuckle, films were not only the road to fame and fortune but also a golden, entirely unexpected opportunity to expand their powers of invention beyond the limits of the stage to a limitless field which, they soon discovered, was that of the universe itself. Exactly how they made this discovery, and the exuberance with which they made it, are well rendered in Lloyd's book—as well as the painstaking artistry they developed: that urge of the early film-makers to, in Lillian Gish's words, make every shot "accurate, true, perfect."

Nowhere else, to my knowledge, is film comedy construction discussed in so much detail. Rudi Blesh's book on Keaton is excellent on Keaton's vaudeville days and on his earliest films, but thereafter strangely peters out. The two other Keaton books, and the innumerable books on Chaplin, fall far short of this first-hand description of comedy film-making, which is also, in its way, a description of the "psychology of the film experience."

How good it would be to have a book devoted to what happened to Lloyd after 1928—his successful passage of the talkie test, his gradual awareness that the tide of taste was running against him, his efforts to adapt and his eventual prudent retirement. As well as some account of his abortive comeback, under the auspices of Preston Sturges and Howard Hughes, in the strange film variously titled *Mad Wednesday* and *The Sin of Harold Diddlebock.*

Contents

List of
Illustrations

* The photographs marked with an asterisk were acquired from Cinemabilia in New York; the publisher is grateful to Mr. Ernest Burns.

Main Street

BIRTH was one of the least interesting things that ever happened to me; but there must be an opening shot in a war, tears at a wedding, a raccoon coat on a sophomore and a birth in a biography, experts tell me.

The Lloyd family lived in seven different authenticated Nebraska and Colorado towns, some of them twice or oftener, in my first fifteen years. The towns were Burchard, Humboldt, Pawnee City, Beatrice and Omaha, Nebraska; and Fort Collins and Denver, Colorado. No two of us can agree, can even reach a compromise, as to the order of these movings, and no one kept a diary; but fortunately for the necessities of biography there is no dispute as to the fact, the place or the time of my birth. The place was a frame cottage in Burchard, a town of 300 in the First District of Nebraska, just then represented in Congress by a young man named William Jennings Bryan. The time was April 20, 1893, a few days in advance of the outbreak of the silver panic and of the opening of the Chicago World's Fair, neither of which events was associated with my birth at the time, or later. The former, however, may very well have left its mark upon me, for a long period of national hard times set in with the panic and the journeyings of the Lloyds began when I was a year old.

In this third paragraph I stop to serve fair warning—or unfair, as you prefer—that I am not a funny man off the screen. In pictures I am as funny as I know how to be, like the job and have no secret sorrows that I am not John Gilbert or Adolphe Menjou; but I have no desire to be or knack for being comic in my off hours. Such comedy as there will be here—and there should be plenty of it—will lie in the humor of events, not in any conscious effort of the author to be cute.

The Lloyds went to Southeastern Nebraska in pioneer times

from Pennsylvania, my grandfather opening a general store in Burchard. My mother, coming out from Toulon, Illinois, to visit Nebraska relatives, met and married my father there. I was the second of two children, five years younger than my brother Gaylord.

The first move from Burchard was only a hop and a skip twenty-two miles eastward along the Kansas City-Denver line of the Burlington to Humboldt, a place of some 1200. All our Nebraska homes, Omaha excepted, were within the First Congressional District. A man named Bennett had picked up a photographer's outfit, head pincers, birdy and all, cheaply in Chicago, moved it to Humboldt and opened a studio. He knew photography but lacked capital; my father had some capital and no photography, so they became the firm of Bennett & Lloyd, Cabinet Photos a Specialty.

It would be a better story if Master Harold Clayton Lloyd, having been exposed to a camera at this early age, had never recovered and sat around drumming his heels thereafter waiting for the motion picture to be born that he might get in front of a camera taking 960 pictures a minute where only one grew before. That was not the way of it. When, at length, I stumbled into pictures it was as a stop-gap at three dollars a day to fill a hungry stomach. The studio at Humboldt was an episode that I know of only by hearsay and the further evidence of a portrait taken by my father which I have reason to fear will be printed along with this text.

The photographic adventure was not a success and we moved next to Denver, where my father clerked in a shoe store. On the theory that anything that is worth telling is worth telling accurately, a family council was called at the beginning of this task in the hope of agreement on an authorized and official version of our route. Up to our first arrival in Denver, my father, mother and brother agree; thereafter there are three accounts which cross and recross one another. One has us moving from Denver to Fort Collins, back to Denver, thence to Pawnee City, returning to Denver; next to Beatrice, thence to Omaha, once more to Denver and back again to Omaha. It will do as well as another; the point is that we moved. Father and mother admit that we moved; they protest only that we were not so continuously in motion as I remember.

Perhaps not, but this restlessness was not so unusual as it sounds to-day. The same dissatisfactions and optimisms that sent the pioneers across the Mississippi in search of a promised land kept many of them moving when the grass turned out to be not so green as it first had seemed. The population was in a constant state of being shuffled and reshuffled.

It still goes on; nearly 1,000,000 persons have moved to Los Angeles since I first came here.

There are two kinds of poor boys in America—the Tom Sawyers and the Huckleberry Finns, and Hollywood is full of examples of each who have reached the top in pictures. If you remember your Mark Twain, Tom's family was the kind that used to be described as poor but honest. That is, they were self-respecting; and, in a place where all were poor, suffered no penalty for poverty. Tom was young Sammy Clemens himself. Huckleberry was the kid from across the tracks whose lawless life Tom envied. His family was shiftless and not altogether respectable, as well as being poor. They usually were described as white trash.

The mammas of the old home town unanimously predicted a bad end for the Huckleberries, and the Huckleberries frequently defied the mammas and environment and grew up to be first-rate citizens. It would be easy to make this more exciting by putting myself down as a Huck Finn, but it would not be true. I was a good example of a Tom Sawyer. As people went in the West, we were not poor; my father was better off than most of his neighbors, to begin with, for he had a little capital. But as others grew moderately prosperous with time, we slipped back a little, until we were, in the United States sense of the word, poor. In our lowest ebbs I went to live with various aunts and grandmothers, and my schooling went on, interrupted only by the intervals of moving.

These visits further complicate the question of where and when. For example, the family never lived in Durango, Colorado, but I did on two occasions. So when I tell a story as happening in Beatrice or Omaha or Denver, I tell it as I remember and do not guarantee the time or place.

My argument, if I haven't lost you, is that I was average and typical of the time and place. Supposing Atlantic City had been holding Average American Boy contests, with beauty waived, I might have been Master America most any year between 1893 and 1910. This is assuming that the average boy before the war was moderately poor, that his folks moved a good deal and that he worked for his spending money at any job that offered.

In two things I was exceptional—freckles and a single-tracked ambition. Authors always make their boy heroes red-haired and freckle-faced, and you may suspect the freckles were double exposure. Wrong. My hair is black, but I was as freckled as Wesley Barry. Though much dimmed by time, they can be seen yet. As to ambition, I cannot remember ever of wanting to be an engineer, fireman, policeman, bakery-wagon driver or any of the other pre-Lindbergh goals of boys. As far back as memory goes, and to the exclusion of all else, I was stage crazy. There is no accounting for its strength and persistence, for it began before I ever saw a play, and there were no actors, so far as we know, in either my father's or mother's family.

Gaylord was bitten by the same bug less severely, but long before he got his first job backstage I already was playing theater, with the loose hats and caps in the house as my actors. We lived in a duplex apartment, an aunt living across the hall. She owned a large couch, probably one of those trick furnitures that double by day as a davenport and by night as a bed. It was my stage. Taking off my shoes, which was required by my aunt, I would sit tailor fashion on the couch with the hats ranged in front of me. I invented and spoke their lines and moved them about. Of the plays, I remember only that they were as full of violence as Shakspere's own. This was a regular diversion, they tell me. I recall the game better at a time when hats ceased to satisfy my critical sense and were replaced by false faces left over from Halloween. From masks I graduated into real make-up before my teens.

In other matters I had a family reputation of being fickle. For instance, I had a succession of hobbies, each ridden furiously for a time, then abruptly tossed aside forever; but through all I played actor, and at the first opportunity became one.

That is well ahead of my story, however. Before the stage claimed me—or, more precisely, I claimed the stage—for good, I held more assorted boy jobs than a stock actor plays parts in a season. Not that there will be any order to these kid recollections. I put them down ramblingly, much as they come back.

The excuse for putting them down is that they describe pretty accurately an average American Boy.

It was about the time of the hat-and-cap theater that I first ran off. That is what it was called, though it seems to have been no more than an unauthorized excursion. I was about five, and with a boy my age strayed to the Platte River. We investigated its stone-skipping and stick-floating possibilities and, following downstream, came to a paper mill, where we spent most of the day. No one appears to have asked us our business; probably we were taken for an employee's kids. Certainly we went into the processes of paper making most thoroughly, for I remember bringing home a sample of the pulp in each of the stages of manufacture. After the paper mill, we explored a lumber yard; then, dusk coming on, hooked on the rear of a South Denver street car. The car happened to stop at our corner, and on the corner brother Gaylord was waiting with that message that always is the same:

"Young man, you're going to catch it."

I think I was forgiven, but a second time it happened I was haled before a sterner judge. We ran away in the opposite direction this time, to the Colorado state capitol. It was a long way from South Denver and we hooked passage on various wagons. There is a museum in the basement of the capitol. As I recall it, it consists largely of mineral specimens, and what interest it could have had for two five-year-old tourists I can't say, yet we went over it case by case. The capitol sits on a knoll, its terraced lawns inclining sharply. We were having a high time rolling down these grassy grades when Aunt Grace came down the street in her pony cart, hauled by Cricket. She was bound on a shopping trip, and so startled at seeing her nephew rolling on the state-house lawn, five miles from home, that she pulled Cricket back on his haunches, then yanked me out of the capitol grounds, and delivered me at my grandmother's, where I got what used to be known as what Paddy gave the drum.

Gaylord says it was Denver, but it seems to me to have been Pawnee City that I tagged him skating. He drove me back, but mother made him take me. I was too young for skating and was put alongside a bonfire while the big boys played shinny. The shinny kept them warm and the fire was neglected. I had not the gumption either to keep it going or to go home. Occasionally

I would whine "How soon are we going home?" and would be told "Pretty soon." When the shinny game broke up I was discovered to be cold-storaged. When Gaylord got me home he got the licking and I got baby-talk sympathy, for my feet were so nearly frozen that they did not return to normal for a day.

Gaylord redeemed himself the following summer by dragging me out of the swimming hole when I was drowning. I remember what every man remembers of the swimming hole—the race to shed your clothes, with "Last man in's a crybaby"; the muddy slide down the bank; the smacking of two rocks together under the water while some kid was diving, thereby nearly breaking his ear-drums; the pelting with mud of any weak sister who tried to dress ahead of the gang; the tying of the other fellow's shirt into hard knots, then wetting it until only teeth and time would unknot it, technically known as "chaw beef."

The worst licking I ever took is associated very definitely with Pawnee, and it was not at the hands of a relative. It was the fourth grade, and in marching out of the room the boys and girls filed down opposite stairs which joined at the landing. At the landing one day I found myself paired off with a girl I didn't like and I broke ranks rather than march with her. After recess the teacher called me to the front of the room and ordered me to hold my hand out. As she struck with a ruler I jerked my hand away instinctively, the ruler hit the desk and broke in half. That was put down as open insubordination and reported to the principal, a man, who kept a black-snake whip for such cases. He expressed a desire to see me in the hall. When he laid on the whip I squirmed, and in trying to hold me he tore the shirt off my back. In this condition I ran home, outraged and yelling. My furious mother took one look and marched upon the school-house demanding an apology. According to family tradition, she got it.

It was at Beatrice that I first stayed up to see the circus come in. Circuses always are due at two A.M. and never arrive until daybreak. Smart boys know this and set the alarm clock; green ones try to stay up. When we no longer could keep one eye open between us, we went to sleep on the lawn of the Rock Island station; but, the dew coming on, we were driven inside to the hard, partitioned depot benches. After a night as long as an

Eskimo ever knew, the circus train rolled in and all of us got the immemorial job of watering the elephants. We began by carrying the water in buckets from a pump. This making no more impression than an eye dropper, we borrowed circus tubs and carried them, slopping at every step, for what seemed hours. Whether that thirst ever was slaked I do not know, for I quit in disgust and began looking for a likely spot to crawl under the canvas, when I found Gaylord carrying boards for the seat-erecting crew. I picked up a board, fell in line and got my pass.

One way of earning money was to scour the alleys for bottles, old iron and discarded washboards and sell them to the ragman. Swimming holes in Denver were apt to dry up in summer and there were no free public pools then, but there was a natatorium near the capitol, where, every Wednesday afternoon, the management would toss five dollars in nickels in the pool, a handful at a time, to be dived for. If the alley harvest was good, we would walk the five miles to the nat on Wednesdays.

The day I recall in particular there were three of us and just enough money to pay our way in. We dived like South Sea Islanders, but never a nickel fell to one of us. The jitney shower was over, our eyes were bloodshot from staring under water and we had given up despondently when some one tossed in a white door knob. I dived for it out of habit, and right beside it on the tank bottom I saw a coin. It looked like a dollar to my eyes, though it proved to be only an overlooked five cents. I began yelling before I came to the top. My lungs were full of water when I reappeared, but I held the nickel high in one hand where all could see. We piled into our clothes and went out to spend it. Across the street was a store where it bought half a dozen sugar doughnuts. Sugar doughnuts, if you do not know, are as large as a pie; the joker is that, like cotton candy, they are mostly air. Six were a sound nickel's worth, at that, and the day was perfect.

Boys gather naturally in gangs. Not far away from one of our Denver homes was a tough bunch and no mistake about it, called the Colfax Gang, and gang fights with rocks and fists were no tea parties. The kids in our neighborhood called themselves the Tenth Avenue Gang in imitation of the Colfax clan, and liked to think they were bad actors. To prove it to themselves they crossed the dry bed of the Platte one day and took on another gang. I was too young for membership in the Tenth Avenues, but I tagged along as camp follower. Surprising and outnumbering the enemy two to one, the Tenth Avenues were winning a glorious victory, when out of nowhere swarmed the enemy's reserves.

My heroes fell back behind a string of moving vans and checked the first onslaught. I did not stay to see the outcome, but fled for home for all I was worth. When I got there no one was at home and I was so scared that I locked the doors and pulled down every blind, although I had put the battle far behind me. Later the running fight went by our house, I peeking gingerly out from behind a shade to watch. Victory went to the heads of the gang from across the river, and they made the tactical error of pressing the routed remnants of the Tenth Avenues into the territory of the Colfax Gang. At this effrontery the Colfax gorillas called out a corporal's guard and swept the invaders back across the river like chaff.

The first nickname to fasten on me was Yabble. No, it is not a typographical error. Moreover, it came about very naturally. A lost pup followed me home in Pawnee. By the time the owner was identified, the dog and I were so fond of each other that he refused to separate us. The pup's name was Bill, and when I called him it was: "Here, Bill! Yah, Bill! Yahbill! Yabble! Yabble!" Some boy with a keen ear pinned the name on me and it stuck as long as we lived in Pawnee.

The pup was a mastiff and grew up to be a whopper. I took him to Durango and there a dog hater fed Bill ground glass in meat. The dog moped for a few days, then toppled over dead. I don't hear of them any more, but twenty years ago it seemed to me that nearly every town included a man or woman with such an insane horror of dogs, any dog and all dogs, that periodically they set out poisoned food until the town was in an uproar, every house that did not harbor a dog was suspected and cat-owning spinsters were under special surveillance. Bill gave me a love of big dogs that has resulted nowadays in my breeding great Danes and St. Bernards, which are about as large as dogs come, and I am a little crazier about them than I was as a boy.

Another memory of Pawnee is of being baptized by immersion. It followed a revival conducted by a traveling evangelist which

Harold, as photographed at the age of three in his father's studio.

Harold Lloyd *in propria persona,* about 1928.

Wearing the lensless glasses which make him a world-famed character.

Harold's father, J. Darsie ("Foxy") Lloyd at the time of his marriage.

Harold and his mother, about 1928.

"Speedy" and "Foxy"
reading fan mail.

Gaylord and I attended regularly. On the appointed Sunday we came in our usual clothes, joined the baptismal party, walked down a flight of steps into a tank built into the church, bobbed under the water, and ascended another flight of steps, at the top of which we were wrapped in blankets.

One of the hobbies which raged violently was marbles. I did not tire of them until I had become the ward sharpshooter and had corralled all the prize agates for blocks around at keeps. My sentimental father, who always has put away and preserved my trophies as I tired of them, still has a collection of some seventy agates that I once led captive. Though I never played again, I can't resist a choice agate to this day and I buy them for Mildred's small brother. In the collection was an unusual blue agate with a white bull's eye. I still keep an eye out for its mate.

The capital-H hobby was tricks and magic. It began with an absorption in puzzles in Sunday papers and boys' magazines, then mechanical puzzles. Whether I first read of tricks in advertisements in these papers and sent away for them, or first saw them in the downtown novelty store in Denver while buying puzzles, I can't say; but I went at them with that whole-souled devotion that characterized all my enthusiasms, and didn't live them down completely until two years ago. Even after marriage I continued to carry a pocket stuffed with pocket tricks and was a parlor pest, likely to extract an egg from my hostess' mouth at any lull in the conversation. The tenacity with which the craze hung on can be explained, no doubt, by its close association with the theater; for, if I am not mistaken, I once thought of taking up magic professionally, and I continue to be a member of the Society of Magicians, though of strictly amateur status.

An early piece of apparatus, at a time when we lived near City Park, Denver, was what was called a plate mover. It consisted of a thin rubber tube with a squeeze bulb at one end and a smaller deflated bulb of thin rubber at the other. To test it out I invited another boy to dinner, first running the tube under the tablecloth and fixing the deflated bulb under the guest plate. Albert came, awkward with the double embarrassment of being in the company of strange grown-ups and his mother's warning to watch his table manners. We had chops, and every time Albert got his knife and fork into carving position I squeezed the bulb and the plate leaped up. With each buck his nervousness grew until tears of mortification came to his eyes. Little Harold could keep a poker face, and the rest of the family knew nothing of what was going on. When Albert's plate was changed I contrived to slip the bulb under his coffee cup, and when this, too, began to prance, it dawned on Albert that something was rotten in Denver. Knowing that, he knew all.

I had read *Tom Sawyer*. Whether the idea came from the book, or whether Tom's fence-whitewashing gag is the sort of thing that springs instinctively to boy minds, I don't know, but I worked a variation of it in Durango. I was paying a visit to Aunt Grace and had been told to clean up the back yard. It looked like a long job, a dirty one and uninteresting, so the kids of the neighborhood did it for me. They did it under a contract whereby I explained one trick for a given stint of work, and my repertoire of magic was a large one by then.

The paraphernalia included a marked deck of playing cards. There was a bicycle lamp in two of the corners and the gimmick, as magicians say, was that the shading of the lamps revealed the suit and number of each card. Sometime earlier I had seen *Alias Jimmy Valentine*, dramatization of the O. Henry story wherein the reformed crook sandpapers his fingers to a sensitiveness that permits him to feel the workings of the tumblers of the vault lock in which the child accidentally has been shut, thereby exposing his criminal past in order to save the child. "Is this quite clear? Well, no matter," as Charles Brackett says.

There was a new boy in the block and he pestered me to know the secret of seeing through the backs of cards. It was an exquisite sense of touch, I explained, a delicate perception which could be obtained only by sensitizing the fingertips—for example, by rubbing them to a fine edge on the sidewalk. In one lesson it was possible that he might be able to distinguish between the red and black cards; to equal my gift of calling the suits, even the exact numbers, naturally would require long application and possibly special aptitude.

We were sitting on the cement steps of my grandmother's home in Durango and the new boy began rubbing his fingers on the concrete. In calling the colors the odds were even, so he frequently got two, three, even four cards in succession right, only to fail as many times in a row. When successful, he glowed and commanded our admiration; when he failed, he gave his fingertips a further scouring on the steps until they were nearly as raw as Jimmy Valentine's were supposed to be, and we took pity on him. Pity did not include a true explanation, however; tricks were not given away for nothing.

A like trick of boyish cruelty was played on a youngster in Burchard, where I had gone to visit my father's mother. A hypnotist came to town, and I, as I shouldn't have to tell you by this time, was in the audience. Hypnotism still was a vogue and no opera-house season was complete without one. Burchard was a one-night stand, but where the show played a week the professor would put a man or a woman to sleep in a bed smack in the front window of the best furniture store, and boys lost sleep trying to catch the subject taking food or exercise. There was one hypnotist playing the Missouri Valley country who, instead of putting his subject to sleep in the show window, would bury him alive in a coffin at the conventional six-foot depth and dig him up after twenty-four hours, which, any fair-minded reader should admit, is a good trick if you can do it.

Such troupes carried their own plants, but always hired a group of town boys for added comedy. Certainly any bright boy or girl need not be told that I was one of those boys. We were paid a dollar apiece and were cautioned by the professor:

"Now, boys, I may not hypnotize all of you; but remember I am paying you money and don't spoil my show." We understood.

When the curtain was up and the short opening lecture on mesmerism concluded, we were called to the stage as presumable volunteers. The professor stared us in the eyes, made his passes, then the monkey business began.

"Boys, you are in a strawberry patch," he said with a wink to the audience. "Now you are eating to your hearts' content. These are particularly fine berries and you haven't had any for a long time. Eat hearty! Ah, now you are getting the stomach ache."

We went through the pantomime of picking and gobbling the fruit and at the proper moment we doubled up in convincing distress.

We were told that we were monkeys—monkeys moreover that were troubled with fleas—that we were roosters at daybreak, and we scratched and crowed and flapped our hands. He gave us each a chair which he said was a horse and commanded us to race across the stage, and we raced. The audience enjoyed it, we enjoyed it and the professor enjoyed it.

The fact that none of us was quite sure whether the others really were hypnotized or were just playacting as we were, made it more exciting.

The next day in my grandmother's yard I held court and told all comers all about it. To a small boy named Herrin I boasted that, what's more, the professor had imparted the secrets of the hypnotic art to me. The boy demanded that I prove it by hypnotizing him. For reasons of my own, I preferred to reverse the order.

"That wouldn't do you any good," I argued plausibly. "When you're hypnotized you don't know what you're doing and you wouldn't believe it when you came out. I'll teach you how to hypnotize me instead."

He was shown the mesmeric stare, the passes of the hands and, finally, the finger snapping that brought the subject out of his trance. He was an apt pupil and I a splendid subject, a trance resulting immediately. For half an hour he had me cavorting around the yard supposedly at his will, and how he enjoyed it! I was older and bigger, yet he was my master. When he no longer could think of anything more to order me to do he snapped his fingers to end the entertainment, but the subject failed to snap out of it. He snapped his fingers again, he experimented with other fingers, waved his hands, commanded, coaxed, pleaded, pretended to go home and leave me, to return again to more finger snapping. My uncle John came home to luncheon to find all the snap gone out of Master Herrin's fingers and the boy nearly hysterical, but Uncle John had the family liking for horseplay and insisted that he was powerless. I was one to squeeze the last drop out of any joke, but when the boy broke into sobs his subject began to rub his eyes and manifest other signs of returning consciousness.

One of my first jobs was in a branch milk depot in Denver. In the morning I rode on the delivery wagon as the driver's helper. From noon until three P. M. I substituted in the depot for the clerk. As a side line there was a soft-drink stand and candy case in the depot and that was the true explanation of why I was working there.

The milkman knew his boys. "Help yourself, bub, and don't

be bashful," he told me. With a little time out for waiting on customers, I shook milk shakes and sampled the candy continuously from twelve to three for two days. The third day and thereafter I shuddered at the sight of "red hots" and at the mention of vanilla. Later I had a summer job in a neighborhood drug store in Omaha. I was errand boy, bottle washer, pill-box filler and self-appointed apprentice to the soda jerker. When the latter failed to come to work one day I was promoted to his white apron and it was the milk depot all over again for a short and sirupy spell; then the boss' ice creams and fruit juices were as safe with me as his castor oil.

Aside from jobs around theaters, of which I held many, my early contacts with big business included being a telegraph messenger boy in Omaha, apprentice in a blueprint shop, boy in a bird store, cleaning cages, filling the seed and water cups and contracting a permanent distaste for the society of our little feathered friends; stockroom boy in the chinaware department of Bennett's department store in Omaha; cash boy in Daniels & Fisher's big store in Denver; selling peanuts, pop corn and crackajack in both the Omaha and the Denver Western League baseball parks, and carrying paper routes in Omaha, Denver and Durango. I never formally took up elevator piloting, but Gaylord ran many of them, and when I had no job of my own he would let me sit in for him in slack hours. All were summer or part-time jobs.

There were only two jobs that gave me any sound business training. One was a paper route. In Omaha I carried the Bee, and at another time the World-Herald; in Denver it was an afternoon paper with a Sunday-morning edition—I am not clear which one. In Omaha the carrier was merely a delivery boy, but in Denver I owned the route and discovered responsibility and initiative. By the Denver system the route owner was a middleman between the publisher and the householder. I bought my papers outright at wholesale and sold them at retail just as the street newsboy does. The route was a piece of property, a franchise within a certain territory in the City Park region. If I built it up, the profit was mine; if I failed to collect the accounts, the loss was mine. I had to keep my own books, and if a customer did not pay promptly I stopped his paper without consulting any one.

It is strange that there are men and women who would

deliberately cheat a paper boy, yet there always were homes from the steps of which the paper vanished nightly but where the door never was answered on collection days. I used to come on odd hours and odd days, and when that failed I'd punch the front doorbell and run to the back door, but there is no strategem that will make a dead beat pay a paper boy's bill if shame won't do it. The route was run down when I bought it. I built it up until I had two boys working for me, and sold it at a profit when we moved again. While I carried it I was going to the East Denver High School, taking care of neighbors' furnaces of winter mornings and cutting their lawns in summer.

The other job that returned me something more than a few dollars was of my own devising. We were living in Beatrice, where my mother had a millinery shop and I was going to school. From watching the news butchers on the trains I got the idea of selling pop corn on my own. I bought the corn, bought a stack of sacks at wholesale from a local paper house, made a cut-rate deal with the grocer for butter, and promised my mother a percentage on sales if she would pop the corn. At noon, with two loaded market baskets, I would make the Burlington station and a through train due at that hour. The train carried a news butcher who made forcible objection to my competition, but he never overtook me. After school I made the Rock Island and Union Pacific stations and a regular route that included the public library at one end of the social scale and eight saloons at the other, with an iron foundry in between. Regrettable to relate, the pop corn sold best in the saloons, where its saltiness made it a competitor of pretzels with the beer drinkers.

I had the sales sense to keep the merchandise and myself spick and span, and netted from twelve to fifteen dollars a week, with which I bought all my clothes and started several savings-bank accounts which never lasted until the first interest date. Another move ended the job.

I really shouldn't tell this story; the man hasn't taken a drink in years and I wouldn't hurt his feelings for anything. No one will identify him, but unfortunately he may recognize himself. The only excuse for bringing it up after all these years, aside from the fact that it is funny, is that it contributes its bit to the pictures we are trying to draw of a boy growing into responsibilities.

To prevent confusion we shall have to invent a name for him and call him, say, Joe Morgan. He was an old family friend and had stopped in Denver on his way to Colorado Springs to build himself up physically after taking a cure. Colorado Springs is a pleasant place and he suggested that Harold come along as company. That being agreeable to all, especially Harold, we boarded a D. & R. G. train.

In Denver, Mr. Morgan had been militantly sober, but before the train stopped at Palmer Lake for luncheon he had bought a bottle of whisky from the train porter and soon was limp with liquor. There is nothing funny about a man's fight against such a disease, and I am not trying to make it so, but the consequences may be ridiculous. Though I was not more than thirteen, I think, I knew enough to go through his pockets and confiscate most of his money. Colorado Springs was strange to me, so I bundled my responsibility into a cab and told the driver to take us to a good hotel.

Undressing him, putting him to bed, locking the door, hiding his clothes in the floor linen closet and confiding in the clerk and bell boys, I went forth to see the city. The Seven Falls and Cheyenne Canyon trip was recommended highly. I rode a burro up the canyon and back in what was laughingly called a race with other tourists, and returned to the hotel to find that Morgan had waked, tried to force, cajole and bribe his way out of the locked room and had been ignored by the hotel staff. He was sober and docile when I unlocked the door, and he let me understand that I had acted with a wisdom beyond my years.

We went out to dinner. I ordered a steak and potatoes, he only a cup of coffee, apologizing that he was not feeling too robust.

He toyed with the coffee for a time, then said: "Harold, I think I need a little air; I'll just step out front and wait for you. Don't hurry."

Harold's mind was not entirely free of doubts. I watched with one eye while my host strolled back and forth in front of the restaurant with an elaborate casualness. His beat carried him out of my sight momentarily at each end, but his reappear-

ances were as regular as a pendulum, and Harold became en-
grossed in steak and potatoes. As the stopping of a clock to
which your ear is used makes a louder noise than its ticking, so
the fact that Mr. Morgan was overdue on his return trip
penetrated to me. I dashed out the door, yelling to the cashier
that I would return, and looked down the street to see Morgan
just vanishing into a drug store. Following on the run, I found
him in whispered consultation with the druggist.

Colorado was a wet state, but Colorado Springs was dry. Gen.
W. J. Palmer, founder of the town and builder of the Denver
and Rio Grande Railroad, had written into the city's charter
and into the title to every foot of land a perpetual prohibition
against the sale of liquor within the corporation limits. Probably
I knew nothing of this, but I knew something of bluffs.

"If you sell whisky to this man I'll report you to the police,"
I warned the druggist. The latter assured me that he wouldn't
think of such a thing, and I led Morgan, abashed but unprotest-
ing, back to the restaurant and did not let him out of my sight
that evening.

The next morning I woke with the sun, keen for more sight-
seeing and unwilling to waste an hour of daylight. It is one thing
to lock a drunken man in his room and hide his clothes, another
so to outrage a sober man who only is to be suspected of an
intention to get drunk. So I compromised. I hid his shoes, but
hid them in the room, so that, if necessary, I could pretend that
he had mislaid them himself. Then, distrusting the adequacy
of this, I returned and tied the strings in a tangle of knots.

The Cave of the Winds was the objective this day. You rode
a long way on a street car, then took a hack, or walked, as your
pocket suggested. Walking was discouraged by those who made
their living hauling tourists, and when the hot and dusty way-
farer stopped to ask how far the cave was it was a local joke to
tell him "Just around the bend." The road had more bends
than the famous Cripple Creek Short Line itself, and I had turned
half a hundred of them afoot without making any appreciable
progress, when a wagonette drawn by two plodding horses and
driven by a weather-beaten old woman passed upbound.

"How much farther is the cave?" I asked again.

She grinned and said, "Jump in beside me, sonny, and ride;
it's a long ways around the bend."

We were not yet halfway up the canyon, I discovered, and at the head of the canyon there was a long steep grade up the mountain. Then when we arrived there was a large sign reading "Admission $1." I had sixty cents, but the masterful old woman browbeat the gatekeeper into letting me in at half rate.

After the stalactites and stalagmites and the long ride back, I found that Joe Morgan had risen, recovered his shoes, snapped the knotted strings and tossed them away, then gone out to drink without the let or hindrance of a meddling, impertinent young brat.

In the morning he was sober again and I proposed a trip to Manitou, with possibly an ascent of Pike's Peak.

"Sure, run along and enjoy yourself. Do you need any more money?" said my host, but I refused to go a step except in his company.

As the street car for Manitou approached Colorado City, which was wet, Morgan cleared his throat and remarked, "Harold, you know what I really need is just one drink. That would clear my head and fix me up. I don't believe I'm equal to the Pike's Peak trip without it."

It sounded plausible, and, though Harold had his misgivings, we alighted. As a minor, I was not permitted inside a barroom. Mr. Morgan told me to wait outside, where he would rejoin me almost at once.

Once behind the swinging doors, he knew he was safe and he enjoyed his little joke up to the hilt. I did sentry duty outside, occasionally pushing back the doors just far enough to peer in, see him leaning gustily against the bar and call to him. When he did come out and I got a towline on him, he was roaring drunk. A street car was out of the question, so I looked for some secluded bench where we could park until he had partly sobered.

The spectacle of a strange boy, objectionably dressed up in knickers, white collar and other prissy apparel, leading a drunken man, invited the jeers of two Colorado City boys of practically no refinement. Their comments finally riled me so that I propped my charge against a dead wall and chased my defamers two blocks. I didn't catch them, neither did they come back, and later in the day I got Morgan back to the hotel.

Knowing when I had enough, I wired to Denver to come and get him. As a moral lesson it was worth ten thousand temperance tracts to a boy. It never was needful to warn me away from the flying hoofs of the Brewers' Big Horses.

Once I was headed for the prize ring, thought seriously of taking up fighting professionally, but my mother put her foot down. I always have been fast and shifty and seem not to remember a time when I was not familiar with boxing gloves. It may be that Gaylord had a pair and taught me a little or that an early Christmas brought me a pair.

The name Harold used to be—maybe is yet—in low repute with kids. It was supposed to be sissy and its possessors frequently had to defend it with their fists, though I recall no trouble on this score. I did pick up a few rudiments of boxing very early, however, and was several jumps ahead of the average boy my age.

Once I went to visit my cousin Ray at Wilcox, Nebraska. It was winter and the village hangout was the back of a barber shop, where a pot-bellied stove glowed red and a set of gloves hung on a nail. The loafers would entice youngsters inside and match them in bouts.

A city kid normally is a shining mark in a country town; but as the owner of a straight left I won the barber-shop belt so quickly and easily that the sporting element looked about for sterner stuff to trip the city boy, and found him in a lad named Dave Wright. The bout was staged behind the grain elevator and drew a crowd. How long it went is not of record, but it was long enough. The decision was a draw and I was well satisfied.

Back in Denver, I decided to take boxing lessons and enrolled at Jacobs' gymnasium in Curtis Street. The teacher, a grizzled old pug, tall and slender, taught me the one-two, not to telegraph my blows, improved my left and was making a boxer of me. It was all in the day's work with him and he went through his part of it bored and mechanically.

Becoming excited, I got my routine mixed and struck out of turn. His guard was down, the blow caught him on the jaw and bowled him over. Retired pugs do not appreciate being smacked down by a green youth and he was furious. My apologies were profuse and sincere, however, and he let it pass.

At another time I got my come-uppance, and inexcusably. A professional wrestler, a grown man, worked out at the gym. Seeing me shadow-boxing one afternoon, he asked, "Want to put on the gloves with me, kid?" Anxious to learn wherever I could,

I agreed eagerly. We sparred lightly for a time, then he deliberately uncorked one from his shoestrings that knocked me to the far wall of the gym and left me bruised for several days. The wrestler grinned, tossed off his gloves and went to the showers.

There were Sunday afternoon smokers at Jacobs', where I fought in four two-minute-round bouts with other pupils. Jacobs entered his students in the Denver Athletic Club city amateur championship tournaments and I was training for one of these when my mother intervened. I had sold her on the idea that it was well for a boy to know the manly art of self-defense, but this was getting too professional for her tastes. The boy who won the D. A. C. championship in my class I had whipped before and whipped afterward, so it is not unlikely to suppose that I would have been a Denver amateur champion, and, had I gone that far, certainly I should have wanted to go farther.

A little later, when I went to Durango from Denver, a high-school freshman, I found that the school champ was a husky Negro boy. There was a gym in the school basement and boxing gloves were part of the equipment. The colored boy had a weird and terrifying style that baffled his local opponents, but was just sound and fury to a run-of-the-mill boxer. He never laid a glove on me and I won another championship—my last. I had my eye on a different platform.

II

The Meanest Cowboy
of the West

A BOY born since 1910 can no more name his first movie than
he can remember his first motor car. Memory dawns for him
in a world filled with both. The first picture I ever saw was
The Great Train Robbery, a famous very early American film,
and it is no great feat of memory to recall it. It was the first plot
ever filmed and it introduced to the screen a vaudeville actor,
Gilbert M. Anderson, later to be known as Broncho Billy.

A medicine show came to Pawnee City. Medicine shows—and
there are as many to-day as ever—were like church socials in
that it cost nothing to get in but something to get out. The
entertainment ranged from a black-face banjoist on a high pitch
on the street to a full-length dramatic stock company performance under a big tent where the doctor sold his herb tonic and
snake-oil liniment between acts.

This was about 1902 and the moving picture yet was a novelty.
In many of the smaller towns one never had been seen, and it
was a stroke of showmanship on the part of the med doctor to
buy a worn copy of this early film. Draping a sheet from the
second-story windows of a building across the street from his
pitch, he would project the film on the sheet, attract his push,
as a pitch man calls his crowd, then depend on his native
eloquence to do the rest. As it was tacitly understood that kids
had no money and would not be so silly as to spend it for
medicine if they did have it, med doctors were rated as public
benefactors by us. In return the docs tolerated our noisy and
unprofitable presence, not only because they couldn't help it
but because they knew we were their best advertisers, spotting
their arrival instantly and spreading the news as so many Paul
Reveres. Let an adult get fresh and he would be blown out of
the crowd by a blast of heavy sarcasm; for "the kiddies, heaven

bless them," a set and patient smile was kept.

The scene in *The Great Train Robbery* where the masked bandit crawled over the coal tender and stuck the revolver in the face of the engineer is as clear as if I had seen it last week. In Denver later, and still later in Omaha, much of my money went to nickelodeons, where two pictures made a show and the usual picture was half a reel—never more than one reel. If I had a quarter I went to five shows in an afternoon. Most of the films were French, comedy chases made by Pathé, a house that was to distribute my pictures long afterward. The recipe was a misunderstanding which would set the gendarmes in pursuit of the comedian over and through as many obstacles as the director could think of. Frequently the films were reversed after the first showing, defying the laws of gravitation. If it was comic to see a posse of French cops chase the funny man over a high wall, it was much funnier to see them fall up instead of down.

Years before the vitaphone and movietone I saw and heard talking pictures in Omaha. Stationed behind the screen, where they were invisible yet could follow the action of the film, were a man and woman. The man made up lines for all the male characters, the woman for her sex. Both changed their voices to suit, rattled dishes, slammed doors, answered the telephone and were as busy as a jazz-band trap drummer in flannel underwear. The effect was more novel than electrifying.

Pictures, however, were just another form of something to do, falling somewhere between the Sunday comic sections and running to a fire. They had no reality. I never associated them with so romantic a place as the theater and did not think of the actors as beings, but as puppets, as if they had been drawn by one of those rapid-fire sketch artists.

As early as Pawnee the discovery was made that there were jobs for a boy around a theater. In return for opening and closing the lobby door in the hall that served there as an opera house, I was permitted to see the shows, though, like fashionable New Yorkers, I always missed the first curtain. The first chew of tobacco and this opera house rest side by side in the cemetery of my mind. Pawnee is a county-seat town with a courthouse square, where concerts were given once a week of summer evenings by the town band. Sooner or later intellectual curiosity drives a boy to test his tongue on the sharp edge of chewing tobacco. Another boy and I had arrived at this crossroads of experience together one band-concert evening. We bought a plug of tobacco and sampled it gingerly while sitting on the courthouse lawn listening to the band. The tobacco was rolled under our tongues, then spit out with no more damage than a slight bite.

There was a show at the opera house that night. I acted as lobby doorman as usual; then, with my companion in experimental chemistry, found a seat in the shallow balcony of the hall. The plug came out and each took a noble bite. The first act was laid in a grocery store and there was a Dutch comedian who was, to us, very very funny. We chewed and we laughed until the Dutch comic grew so terribly funny and we burst into such glee that simultaneously we swallowed our tobacco. Neither said anything to the other of this accident, but both of us ceased to laugh. A little later he whispered to me that he didn't think much of the show and believed he would step outside. I replied that I, too, was finding the play a disappointment and would go with him. In fact, I went ahead of him.

Probably this was the only show on which I ever walked out. Whether it was *Mazeppa,* Ole Olson, Yonnie Yonson, Sven Swenson, *Uncle Tom's Cabin, Peck's Bad Boy, The Old Homestead, The Flaming Arrow,* Dockstader's Minstrels or *The Round-up*—from which I came away with a high resolve to learn how to roll a cigarette with one hand as Maclyn Arbuckle did—plays differed from one another only as pies. There were many kinds of pies and all were good.

It was at Beatrice, in *Macbeth,* that I first set foot on the stage itself. A Shaksperean repertoire company, bridging the gap from Omaha to Denver with one-night stands, stopped off for an evening. Such troupes always pick up their supers and children locally. Gaylord, who was prop boy and handy man at the opera house, promptly nominated the kid brother to fill one of the breaches. There are three parts in *Macbeth* which might be played by a boy, and my memory is hazier than usual, but apparently I was Fleance, Banquo's son and witness to his murder, for I recall coming on the left of the stage with a man who seems to have been my father and running off right alone and crying "Help! Help!" I had been drilled that afternoon to continue the cry from the wings; but my voice, which had been vocal enough on stage, froze with embarrassment in the presence of the offstage company and one of them had to take up the cry where I left off.

In intervals when I could not crowd on the stage I sold box candy in the Tabor Grand and the Tivoli, Denver; ushered in many houses, sometimes without pay, becoming head usher in the Omaha Orpheum; at other times was call boy, crying, "Fifteen minutes!" "Overture" and "Curtain!" And when older I served as assistant electrician and grip, or stage hand. Hence I knew my theater from Shakspere to the xylophone players.

The Beatrice performance of *Macbeth* was an incident; the curtain really rose for me one day about 1906 in Omaha, when my eye was taken by the hocus-pocus of an astrologer fortune teller who had squatted in a vacant storeroom downtown and filled the windows with his strange charts. Astrology evidently was new to my ken, and its mysteries so compelling that when the fire wagons poured by in answer to an alarm and the little crowd melted away, I only glanced over my shoulder at the hook and ladder.

When the steamer had passed, concluding the show, only two of us remained in front of the window. The other was an interesting-looking man who was so struck by my superiority to fire-wagon chasing that he spoke of it. We talked and he volunteered that his name was John Lane Connor and that he was leading man with the Burwood Stock Company. If a fire couldn't pull me away from the astrologer's windows, here was something exciting enough to do it.

In the course of more talk, during which I confided that I was crazy to go on the stage and had had a little experience, it developed that Connor was fed up on theatrical hotels and restaurants and was looking for room and board in a private house. Unhesitatingly I invited him to lodge with us. Our house was much larger than we had any need for; I knew we could use the money and so took a chance on my mother's agreement. Thereafter, while he remained in Omaha, Connor lived with us; and when the Burwood company played a bill requiring a boy I was the boy. When more than one boy was needed I supplied others from among my friends.

WE were moving again, this time from Twentieth and Dodge

Streets, Omaha, to 2836 Burt Street. Laverne Manning and I rode on the last van load, dangling our legs from the rear, he seeing me on the way to the foreign parts of Burt Street. Changing neighborhoods is not an unmixed pleasure for a boy. He is an alien, a freshman, with a period of hazing and initiation to undergo before being accepted into the new fold. Timid boys stick closely to the sanctuary of their own yard; bold ones get the agony over with quickly by offering to lick the first boy they encounter—and the second and third, if necessary.

Without raising a finger or leaving our front yard, we were the cocks of the walk before nightfall, levying tribute on all Burt Avenue. Certainly we were showing off, but the effect was unforeseen. I had inherited two clown suits from Gaylord, knew clown make-up and business—which never changes—from close observation of circuses and much practice, and owned the needful properties. Each put on a clown suit and drew on a skullcap made from a white stocking, with holes cut for the ears. I made up Laverne and myself with clown white salve and the orthodox markings—the strips over the eyes, the red crescent on one cheek, the dots, the wide mouth slit and putty nose. Then with big clown shoes, floppy white cotton gloves and a slapstick, we emerged into the front yard and put on an act that was an old story on Dodge Street.

It included all the conventional clown foolery and such bits as shooting the apple from William Tell's head and a cracker from the mouth—both as old as sawdust. In the former, one clown holds an apple on his head, the other fires a popgun and at the same instant the first clown jerks his head just enough to unseat the apple. In the second skit the clown with the cracker between his teeth bites down just as the other fires the popgun and the bulk of the cracker falls from his mouth as if it had been shot out.

The fact that we gave the act in the front yard rather than the back indicates that we hoped for an audience. Normally two boys could not be induced to make such a show of themselves in a strange neighborhood, but make-up and costume have the quality of removing self-consciousness by covering the self. A mask alone will do it, as any masked ball will prove.

A boy came down the street, aimlessly kicking a block of wood, stopped in amazement, then peered timidly through the iron

Assorted adventures of Harold Lloyd: a pot-pourri from his films.

(1) Selling shoes.

(2) Saying a prayer.

(3) Singing a hymn.

(4) **Riding a motorcycle.**

(5) Threading a needle.

(6) Causing consternation.

(7) Losing an automobile.

(8) Cleaning a mirror.

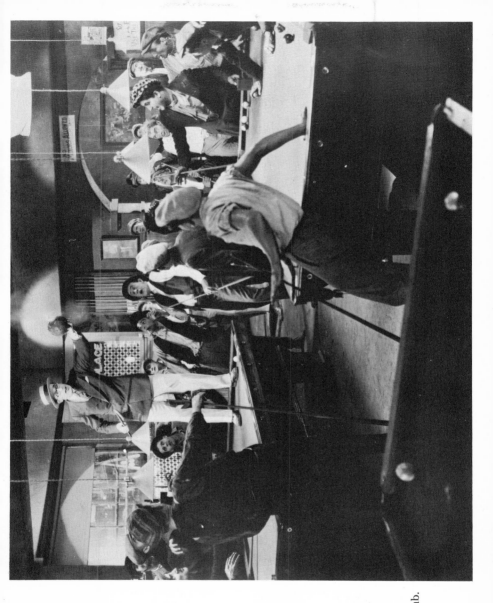

(9) Brandishing a bomb.

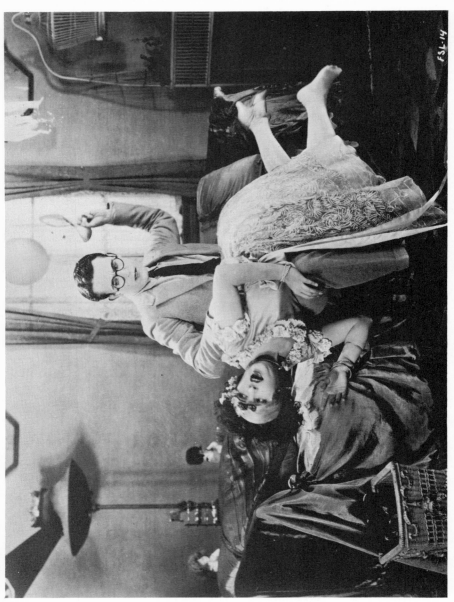

(10) Punishing a lady.

fence, unable to credit his eyes. Two boys farther up the street saw something going on and joined him at the fence; then more, until every kid in the street, two big boys from a passing department-store delivery wagon, an Italian huckster and some of his housewife customers had gathered at the fence. Even when they saw us in ordinary clothes the next day, we were not two more boys to the kids of the block, but authentic clowns that by some special dispensation had come to live in their block, and our society was sought on any terms we might dictate. Most of them were mustered into a backyard and cellar repertoire company soon after.

There had been a stage in the basement of the Twentieth and Dodge house, built for me by father, and he duplicated it in the Burt Street home. The two cellar theaters are badly mixed in memory, but, thanks to the enterprise of an Omaha newspaper reporter and the saving ways of my onetime leading lady, we are enabled here to present the priceless, in a manner of speaking, program of *Tom Morgan, the Cowboy of the West,* exactly as written down by the author, Harold Lloyd, and played in the Burt Street basement at three cents for the first row, two cents for the second row, one cent for the third—and the audience all farsighted.

The clipping from which it is reproduced is dated February 20, 1921, and relates that Mrs. Guy Burcham, who was the Edith Wanderholm—on the program Wenderhome—of the cast, found it with other souvenirs of her pigtail days in a trunk. In some fashion I failed to see the clipping when it was new, but my patient father pasted it in a scrapbook, where I have just found it. It is written in ink in a hand that took no honors either in spelling or writing, and it reads:

CAST

Tom Morgan, the cowboy of the West	*Earl Ketcham*
Big-Hearted Jim	*Frank Fisher*
Happy Holiday	*Malcolm Macharthy*
Joe Luck	*Walter Hitch*
Bert Ailsworth, a tender foot from N. Y.	*Raymond Moore*
Osa Castro, a mexican	*Verne Manning*

Red horse, a indian scout .... *George Noran*

Jack Dalton, the meanest cow
   boy of the West .... *Harold Lloyd*

Sal, a cow girl .... *Edith Wenderhome*

Helen Allisson .... *Margaret Macharthy*

Acts 1-2-3

A SALLON IN DEAD GUCH, COLORADO

Stage carpender .... *Russel Tetard*

Stage director .... *Harold Lloyd*

The casting of myself as the heavy confirms my memory that, let who would be the hero, I chose always to be the villain. Mrs. Burcham recalled, as I do not, that on his first entrance Jack Dalton espied the tenderfoot, Ailsworth, cracked down on him with the pearl-handled revolver and commanded, "Dance, you tenderfoot!" That sounds likely. I do remember, however, that Raymond Moore was a delicate child and accordingly was cast as the effete Easterner, and that Joe Luck was so named because he was a card sharp. Mrs. Burcham recalled the plot as centering around the kidnaping of Helen Allisson by the bad Mexican, Castro, played by Laverne Manning, but she did not say which side Jack Dalton rode with; no doubt it was at the unspeakable Castro's flank. "Dead Guch" is intended, of course, for "Dead Gulch," and the spelling of the true names of the cast likewise reflects no credit on the near-by Webster school.

More informal horse operas were played out-of-doors. Among my growing properties were four or five genuine revolvers—rusty perhaps, but man-sized. Two of them came from Gaylord. I fail to recall the history of the others; but one, reserved for personal use, was long barreled and had a pearl handle. I was not so well equipped as to have blank cartridges. Anyway, the firing was so terrific in our back-yard Westerns that Broncho Billy Anderson couldn't have kept us in blanks.

It was necessary therefore to yell "Bang! Bang!" whenever a trigger was pulled—a most unsatisfactory state of affairs, for cowboys, Indians and bandits alike continued to fire and charge while practically riddled with bangs, owing to never-settled disputes as to who had been shot and put out of action first. With the play threatening to degenerate into a debating society, we had an inspiration. The revolvers were retired to the cellar stage and each of us bought a water pistol. By agreement, one drop of water was sudden death and henceforth the fighting became very much less reckless and spectacular, taking on the nature of ambushes, stalking and sudden forays. The pistoleer had to look to his own supply of water, carrying it generally in a tomato can, and hide it where an enemy could not find it and use it against him.

In the study of make-up I bought a book on the subject in which I remember particularly a photograph of Wilton Lackaye as Svengali in *Trilby*, generally regarded as a masterpiece of make-up. Before I had entrée backstage I carried a notebook when I went to the theater, jotting down such hints as could be picked up from the front of the house. Once backstage, I fastened unerringly on that member of the company who knew the most about make-up, usually the character man, and made myself his slave and yes man. If I had a part of my own I arrived early, was prepared for my entrance before the character man would appear, then stood in his dressing room, studying his technic and asking how and why, this curiosity made tolerable by my lavish admiration and all-around helpfulness.

Inevitably, I became expert. In fact, when Connor boarded at our house I knew already more about make-up than he, an experienced actor, did, for he had played such straight parts as juvenile and leading man almost exclusively. While yet in grade school few effects were beyond me. Crêpe hair comes in braids, and my first accomplishment was the art of unraveling, rolling and shaping it, applying it with spirit gum, then trimming with shears.

Character men taught me how to save a good beard or mustache for future use by applying glue over make-up, the glue coming off with the hair and giving it a good body; how to flatten the nose for Negro or Oriental parts by stuffing rubber tubes in the nostrils; how to build up the face with cotton, collodion over the cotton and make-up over all; how to putty out my own eyebrows and apply brows of a different type; how to make a dead or a grotesque eye by setting half a walnut shell over my own eye, building it into the socket with putty and glue, concealed by flesh paint, then painting the walnut shell to the desired effect; how to set in false teeth over my own; how essential it was to high light all wrinkles, and most of the other tricks of the trade handed down through generations of actors.

If my father saved the Omaha programs with his usual care, my debut with the Burwood company was in *Tess of the D'Urbervilles* in the fat part of Abraham, Tess' little brother. Frank Bacon, who later won immortality in *Lightnin'*, was John D'Urberville, and Lloyd Ingraham, now a well known Hollywood director, was stage manager. The date on the program was January tenth, no year given, but 1907 may be deduced from a clew in a program advertisement.

There must be sixty sides, or pages of manuscript, to the rôle of Abraham and he gets one curtain all to himself. The once noble D'Urbervilles are in a bad way. The landlord is foreclosing and the furniture is being carried away; Abraham lies ill upon a pallet in front of the fireplace and the villain has designs on Tess. She agrees at last to his proposals in order to give little Abe the medical care he must have to save his life. As Tess leaves the house with the heavy, Abraham staggers to his feet, and as she closes the door cries "Tess! Tess!" and falls in a faint at the door. Curtain!

Lloyd Ingraham had schooled me never to step out of character in taking a curtain call. I took it, wan and weak, supporting myself on the knob of the door.

Overeager on the first night, I made my first entrance ten lines too soon and interrupted a tender love passage. Ingraham saw and tore his hair, but, trouper that I was, I drifted backstage to a property wheelbarrow against the back drop, examined it with a counterfeited boyish interest and, as my proper cue approached, picked a property flower, smelled it and dropped it in Tess' lap —all to Ingraham's profound relief. An indulgent critic wrote in the World-Herald:

> The part of Tess' little brother was well done by Master Harold Lloyd, who demonstrated that he has a dramatic instinct which will doubtless carry him on to success in the histrionic art.

I liked it all, especially the "histrionic"—a seventy-five-cent word not yet in my vocabulary.

The next bill, Clyde Fitch's *Lovers' Lane*, called for four boys and I brought with me Laverne Manning, George Norn and

Earl Ketchum, all of whom will be recognized, with some changes in spelling, as veterans of *Tom Morgan, the Cowboy of the West.* On the first Saturday of this engagement I idled about the house, waiting for theater time, and found that the clock had stopped. Out of the door I burst, hatless and running, until the first street car overtook me. No more was I aboard than the car began to act like the clock and move with such agonizing slowness that at the first junction I leaped off and took a car on another route. This motorman, too, at once came down with sleeping sickness and the car crawled, though, from my seat, I pushed with every muscle tensed. I got off and ran again, reaching the theater at last, to find the curtain up on the second act and George Norn playing my part. Right there a career blew up in my face. Unless you have been a boy actor, you can't know the feeling and I shouldn't wish you to. I was cooked. Ingraham took it less seriously, however, and put me on at night as usual.

Several weeks of boyless bills ensued and the next appearance was not until March in *Nell Gwynne,* commemorated by this sentence at the close of a newspaper review:

> As the call boy, Dick, in the theater greenroom scene in the first act, Master Lloyd, who appeared in *Lovers' Lane,* is refreshing and appears perfectly at home despite his youth.

I must have had a press agent.

In *Lovers' Lane,* Frank Bacon was the opera-house manager, with no line to speak and nothing to do, as far as I can recall, but to come out once and paste up a playbill; yet he got the biggest laugh of the show by the way he spit in this paste bucket. All he ever had to do to explode the house was to walk on the stage, and, whatever the character assigned to him, he went on playing Frank Bacon. Audiences would have demanded their money back had he done otherwise. If you saw *Lightnin'*—as who didn't?—you saw Bacon plain, for he and Lightnin' Bill Jones were one and the same. He was a droller character than any he was billed to play. I learned nothing of make-up from him. He did keep two ancient hunks, one red, one black, in his dressing room, but rarely used them. When asked, as he was frequently, what he did with his money, he had one reply:

"I spend it all for make-up."

Nor was make-up the only detail he neglected. He rarely bothered more than to glance at his part, necessitating that his wife, Jane, prompt him from the wings; or, if she happened to be on stage with him, check him in whispers. I had a long scene with him in *Nell Gwynne* and discovered by the second performance that it would be well to learn his lines too.

Mrs. Bacon—Mother Bacon to all of us—scolded him, saying, "Frank, it's bad enough for the grown people, but you at least ought to study your part for the boy's sake."

I saw him backstage in Chicago a few weeks before he died and his greeting was "Up the chimney at Marlowe"—the cue line in *Tess* that he never could remember. It was like him to be letter-perfect in it thirteen years later. At the end of the Burwood season he prepared to take out a vaudeville playlet, expanded eventually into *Lightnin'*. He offered me a part, which my mother declined for me.

At the end of the Burwood season Connor went to Chicago to play at the Bijou. He lived in Ravenswood with his mother and sister, and an invitation coming to me to visit them, mother raised the money to send me, with a side trip to Toulon, Illinois, her old home, where many relatives still lived. There was some confusion as to day, train and station and no one met me in Chicago, which was just as I would have wished it. To meet a boy at a railroad station is to insult him. The larger and more strange the city, the more he rejoices in the sensation of being on his own; and, as his pathfinding sense is much better than the average adult's, to worry over him is to worry over a bad penny. I asked my way of a fat policeman, who said to take an L train and get off at Wilson Avenue, I think it was. Apparently I misunderstood, for I got off many stations too soon and walked miles before I found the Connor home, but I found it and, boy-like, thought nothing of it.

Toulon reminds me that I recall the first automobile ride as clearly as the first movie. I visited around the relative circuit in Toulon for a month, that month including Chautauqua Week, the high spot of any small-town summer. Chautauquas usually are arranged for the benefit of something or other, and this was no exception. As one ingenious means of raising money for the cause, all the automobiles in Stark County—all six of them—were thrown open to public use at five cents the ride. The nickel carried you a round trip of six thrilling blocks from the courthouse and back. My cash balance was twenty-five cents—you know where it went. Before the visit was done a cousin bought an E. M. F., an early American car sometimes affectionately known as the Every Morning Fixit. In this he took me to the neighboring town of Wyoming, where he stopped on business at a store.

"Want to come in, Harold?" he invited.

"No, thanks; I'll just sit out here and wait," said Harold, noting the gathering crowd.

While the populace crowded about, exclaimed and disputed as to whether such devilish contraptions should be permitted on the public roads, Harold sat haughty and silent. It was one of Harold Webster's Thrills that Come Once in a Lifetime—the same Webster who was a cub cartoonist on the Denver Republican when I was a small boy there.

Before going home to Omaha I spent a week at a boys' tent camp at Saugatuck, Michigan, on the lake shore—the only vacation of the kind I ever knew. There were plenty of boys, cherries to steal, Indian trails through dense woods and a botany instructor who taught me trees so well that I still know a little about them.

That summer my voice began to change. No longer fitted for child parts, yet much too young for juveniles, the old career was becalmed. In this awkward pause I resumed ushering and got out the notebook. A young fellow playing an old soldier in an Orpheum act encouraged me; if he could pass as an old man, so could I, and I reapplied myself to make-up. Vaudeville also suggested another alternative. Having lived it down, I can confess that I once had a weakness for dialect and about this time considered equipping myself as a dialect monologuist by a method all my own. The method called for seeking out Irish, German, Jewish and Swedish families with the broadest possible speech and living with each long enough to master their version of English. Once graduated from such a course of study, it looked like I would be fixed for life, with an act requiring only an occasional new story. It was worth a trial, but there must have been difficulties—perhaps family ones.

If this was the fall of 1907, as it seems to have been, a misty interval of nearly four years follows during which we moved several times and I saw the theater only from the front of the house. I know that I divided either the freshman or sophomore year between Omaha, Denver and Durango high schools, and I can fix one date exactly. I was in Durango on July 4, 1910, for I ran the round-by-round reports of the Jeffries-Johnson fight at Reno from the telegraph office to a saloon where they were read. Evidently I returned to Omaha in the autumn, for it was in 1911 that the fortunes of the Lloyd family turned the corner. We moved to San Diego and it was from Omaha that we moved.

That change of fortune was heavily disguised at the moment. For several years my father had been working for the Singer Sewing Machine Company, first as a salesman, then as assistant state supervisor. Sewing machines were the first of all articles, I believe, to be sold widely on the installment plan; also the first generally adopted household labor-saving device. Most women continued to make the bulk of their clothing and the children's clothes, and the market for machines yet was unsupplied. In Omaha father got the nickname of Foxy, which clings to him still. It grew out of his zeal in turning up absconded and only partly paid for machines by examining the serial number of every one he found in use and checking it against a company list. In one day he brought in two long-missing machines, one of which had been sold four years before in New York to a tailor who had moved it first to Denver, then to Omaha.

"Oh, you foxy Lloyd!" the Omaha manager exclaimed, and Foxy he has remained.

In this work dad drove a buggy with a small platform behind capable of holding two sewing machines. He was run down one afternoon by a brewery truck and injured severely. Brewery trucks used to set out in the morning with two racks of full kegs and return in the afternoon with as many empties. It was a saloon convention that when the drivers had shot a loaded keg down the skid into the cellar and wrestled up an empty, the bartender would, without prompting, draw two large steins for the refreshment of the men after their labors, the same being on the house. A generous custom, but resulting sometimes in the truck crew driving breweryward in a beery mist. Such a crew in such a haze ran down dad and his buggy.

After a siege in the hospital and a lawsuit, a jury brought in a judgment of six thousand dollars against the brewery—divided evenly later between the lawyer and father. Such a sum as three thousand dollars suggested a move. Dad was divided between New York, where he never had been, and Nashville, Tennessee, where a relative published a religious journal. New York tempted me, for it meant Broadway; but Connor had moved to San Diego, where he was playing in stock and running a dramatic school, and I sensed that as between the chances of a green boy of eighteen on Broadway and under the wing of such a guide and friend in San Diego, there could be no question of choice. Dad never had seen the Pacific Coast, either, and was open to reason. "We'll toss a coin," he said at last. "Heads is New York or Nashville or where I decide, tails is San Diego."

The coin went up, hit the ceiling, dropped and rolled under a bed. It was a pre-buffalo nickel and it stopped wreath side up. Had it fallen heads, this story would not have been written. The possibilities are infinite; the probabilities are that we would have gone to New York and I would have become a Broadway actor—I hope a good one. Had we turned Eastward rather than West, certainly the odds are long that it wouldn't have been pictures, for I went into pictures only because they were on hand in California when nothing else offered.

In San Diego dad bought a pool hall and lunch counter with his three thousand dollars. Why a pool hall and lunch counter is one of those California mysteries; he knew nothing of either. A passing attack of pool fever in my freshman year in Omaha had left me a good shot, qualified to take a cue for the house any time a house man was called for, but dad had to learn even how to rack the balls. He had neglected, too, to take a tip from chain-store practice and count the pedestrians before he bought. To a stranger in San Diego the location on Grant Park appeared to be ideally central; actually, it was fifty feet off the main traveled path, and only merchants know what a vast distance fifty feet can be.

These are some of the things I did in San Diego: Finished high school; relieved my father in the pool hall and lunch counter; played leads in high-school shows and aided Connor in staging them; acted as assistant in fencing, dancing and elocution in Connor's dramatic school; played in and helped Connor stage lodge and club entertainments; played characters in four local stock companies and was assistant stage manager of one; gave

Shaksperean readings before high-school English and elocution classes; worked as stage hand at the Spreckels, the road-show theater. Many, if not most, of these activities were concurrent.

High-school vogues vary with the schools; in San Diego amateur dramatics were a major activity, nearly on a par in student esteem with football. My first choice naturally would be dramatics, and formal school athletics demanded more time than could be squeezed out of my routine. I had so enormous an advantage over schoolboy amateurs, moreover, that the leading parts fell to me without question, and I came nearer losing my head here than ever before or after. I have many reasons to be grateful to Connor, but the greatest service he did me was to reduce this swelling at the psychological moment.

We gave *Going Some,* a collegiate farce, in the school auditorium on December 6 and 7, 1912—the program, not my memory, is speaking—and I was J. Wallingford Speed, head yeller. By contrast I should have been pretty good. Furthermore, in the training-quarters scene, where the trainer and I held the stage and exhorted the team, the trainer's amateur nose began to bleed copiously. He walked off the stage, leaving me to conduct a monologue, and I got away with it.

I had come back with great relish and yearning to the stage after four years, and, where I had been a humble apprentice among professionals, I was now the fair-haired boy among amateurs. The attack, I suppose, had been coming on for some time and the *Going Some* triumph precipitated it. The next morning I drifted into the dramatic school with my brow bared for the laurel wreath. Connor said hello and went about his business. I stood about waiting for it and when it failed to come I asked for it.

"Not so bad last night, was I?"—or something like that was the prefatory remark.

Connor hesitated as if reluctant to be drawn into so painful a discussion, then said quietly:

"Harold, I was very much disappointed in you. After all, you're not an amateur in his first play—not that I would have known it at times last night. You pulled yourself out of a hole in the training-quarters scene very well, and why shouldn't you? You've been working at the trade for years. On the other hand, how many times have I told you how to get the full value out of a

laugh? Of course you got laughs. The laughs were in the lines
and the situations. Half the time, though, you choked them to
death before they were well started."

Point by point he went over my performance as a mechanic
goes over a motor, pointed out bad timing, wrong emphasis and
other A B C errors of technic. Had he barked "There may be
worse actors than you, but I don't remember one," or some such
blast, he merely would have made me mad and convinced me
that he was jealous of my rising young talent. As it was, my
own experience told me that he was right and just, and my class-
mates must have found me pleasantly improved by the next
school bell. Most boys can use such a jolt to advantage at about
eighteen; a boy actor cries for it.

There had been an incident in *Going Some* which I might
have used as a partial alibi. In a stock-company production of
either *The Bishop's Carriage* or *The Man or the Box* earlier in
the year, I played a butler in the second act and opened as a
police reporter in the fourth, making my change during the
third act. Having missed this act all week, I lingered to watch
it about Friday night and made a hurried change during the intermission. The curtain rose on Act IV with the police reporter
facing the audience, upstage. Titters began to float up from the
front row when no titters were called for; in my hurry I had not
completed dressing. The fear of a repetition haunted me thereafter, so when the prompter began to "Psst! Psst!" from the wings
and to point early in the training-quarters scene, panic took me.
A careful inventory disclosed nothing wrong with my clothing,
but the prompter continued to hiss, grimace and point. Not
until the act was over could I learn that he was warning me
against a handful of tacks left in a chair by the stage crew. The
tacks had gone unnoticed until the curtain was up.

The San Diego programs in dad's scrapbooks are confined to
1912 and are not complete for that year. They record me as
playing in *Doctor Jekyll and Mr. Hyde*, *The Prince Chap*, *Jess
of the Bar Z Ranch*, *Woman Against Woman*, *The House of a
Thousand Candles*, *The Little Minister*, *The Count of Monte
Cristo* and *The Sign of the Four* with Connor and his new Grand
Theater Stock Company; *Salvation Nell* and *A Message from
Mars* in Myrtle Vane's Stock Company at the Savoy, and *The
Aviator* and *Strongheart* in the Metropolitan Stock Company

at the Isis, named and owned by Mrs. Katherine Tingley, high priestess of the Theosophist colony at Point Loma.

By this time Lloyd Ingraham had come to San Diego and was playing with Myrtle Vane. Miss Vane is playing characters in pictures these days. She has a petition in to play my mother in our next picture and we are trying to arrange it. May Robson also is a candidate for the next mother bit. I was one of the Spreckels stage crew when she came to San Diego in 1913 with *The Rejuvenation of Aunt Mary* and fell hopelessly in love both with her and her acting. I shall not let her play my mother, though, and I have told her why; she would steal the picture from me.

The stages of the New Grand and an airdrome, as open-air summer theaters used to be called, were back to back and Charley Ray, who scarcely needs to be identified, was a youngster in the airdrome company at the same time I was one of the Grand troupe. Stella Watts was one of our company. We pondered much over our futures.

"In 1920, Harold, let's put an ad in the Mirror and see what's become of each other," she said one night as we sat out a scene. That sounded like a date in a Jules Verne story. When it arrived the Mirror had suspended, Stella had a single act in vaudeville and I was just beginning to get my head above water in pictures.

These San Diego stock bits all were minor, some more minor than others, and a share of the usual accidents that befall apprentices in the theater went with them. In *Woman Against Woman* I played a valet with no more than six lines, so trivial that I declined to bother learning them. Just before my cue I would glance at the script, stuff the script back into a handy fold in the scenery and go on. I neglected to recover my script after one performance and when next I needed it the set had been torn down and stacked against the back wall with other scenery. In the midst of a frantic and hopeless scramble to find it in time, I heard my entrance cue and instantly remembered my lines.

This is a curious phenomenon of acting. You may have a long part and know it perfectly, yet have your mind go utterly blank as you wait for your entrance. At the height of your alarm the cue line is spoken and automatically your part returns to you as if the drawn shades of a room had been raised in unison. This reaction is so dependable that young actors soon learn not to worry over offstage memory lapses.

In *The House of a Thousand Candles* I played an old sheriff who at one point served a summons on John G.—Griff—Wray. I made my flourishing speech one night, reached for the summons and found that I had forgotten it. "Well, I've got it somewhere," I ad-libbed, and left Wray to do the same while I ducked off stage in quest of any scrap of paper. The audience took it as in character for a comedy sheriff, but at future performances I carried summonses in every pocket.

In San Diego I emerged gradually from that transition stage where I was too old for boy parts and too young for juveniles. While it lasted I drew on my store of make-up lore and played characters, from Tonga the East Indian native who blows the poison darts in *The Sign of the Four* and is ratiocinated to earth by Sherlock Holmes, to old men. Occasionally I was assigned to a type juvenile and once the straight juvenile rôle of Albert in *The Count of Monte Cristo.* Playing straight in a romantic drama demanded carriage, the easy management of a sword and the wearing of a ruffled costume as if one belonged in it. There were no pockets for my hands and I was thoroughly miserable, where as King Lear I would have been entirely at home behind white whiskers and an old man's furrowed face.

When the stock companies closed in late spring and the high school, lodge and club entertainment season ended, Connor organized a circuit stock company to play the surrounding territory on a revolving schedule that gave the company its name. Here I was stage manager, played better parts, even such ambitious rôles as Svengali in *Trilby* and both Fagin and the Artful Dodger in *Oliver Twist,* and got my only real experience in trouping.

At one town on the circuit the only train arrived at six P. M. As stage manager I had to dash for the furniture store, and, if it was closed, find the owner at his home, drag him away from his dinner to unlock the store, select such furniture as the bill demanded, hire a dray to haul it to the theater, set the stage, then make up by 8:15.

Escondido, at the end of a branch railroad line, was one of the towns, and I think it was here that we arrived on the Fourth of July, 1912, in anticipation of a holiday crowd—to see one lone man on the whole length of the main street. There was no celebration in Escondido this year, and the population, we found, had divided itself for the day between Oceanside and another neighboring town, name forgotten, both of which were putting on the usual patriotic carnival. The Escondido manager being agreeable to canceling, we decided quickly to try the town of the forgotten name, having just played Oceanside the day before. Over the telephone we learned that the opera house was not available, so it was Oceanside or nothing and be quick about it.

Much search turned up an old seven-passenger car—probably the only one left in town. Into this piled the twelve of us and our baggage and hit it up for Oceanside, to find the theater there rented for a dance. Heartfelt pleading induced the house manager to persuade the dance promoter to hold his dance after the show. No time remained for the throwing away of dodgers or the usual advertising, so the company made up, then crowded into the car again and toured the streets, ballyhooing. This and the attendance already attracted by the dance filled the house for *Little Lord Fauntleroy,* in which my part was the fat grocer, Hobbs, played with padded coat, a pillow around my waist and cheeks puffed with cotton.

Uncle Tom's Cabin escaped me; but *Ten Nights in a Barroom* was in the repertoire of the circuit troupe, my part Sample Switchell, the village clown—a fat rôle which I made fatter. The script merely indicated the lines, leaving the business to the ingenuity of the actor and permitting a stage hog, such as I was told I was, to build the part up indefinitely. If any prominence remained to Connor as Joe Morgan it was because he fought for it.

The lunch counter and pool hall died in the spring of 1913 after a lingering illness and father went to Los Angeles to look for work, leaving me to finish high school. The school year closed and with it the stock companies and the dramatic school. The circuit troupe was not revived, road shows were infrequent at the Spreckels, Connor was not flourishing and I was too proud to ask his help or any one's. To reduce expenses I moved into a tent on the roof of an apartment house. It was not uncommon in San Diego for an apartment-house owner to erect a tent colony on the roof and let the tents out cheaply as lodgings, as which they did very well in such a climate. There was a day when

I was down to five cents. I bought doughnuts with the nickel, as we had done once in Denver, and the next day *Ben Hur* coming to the Spreckels, I got on for the night as a grip, or stagehand, wages a dollar and a half.

The old Edison company, Laura Sawyer leading woman, Ben Wilson, now a producer, leading man, came out from New York on temporary location in the winter of 1912-13 to do half a dozen pictures. They settled in Balboa, just below Long Beach, and one day in the late spring they made an excursion to San Diego to shoot an atmospheric scene requiring a number of extras as Indian background. They applied at the Connor school, I enlisted, made up as a three-fourths-naked Yaqui and served a tray of food to the white man's party in one fleeting scene. That was my debut in pictures. The three dollars pay, however, was more significant at the moment.

I had not worked for days when a play called *The Bird Cage,* by Austin Adams, opened at the Spreckels and I landed a run-of-the-engagement job as stage manager. Louis Morrison, who had been associated that season with the Grand theater company, directed the play. A stage manager's jobs are many, among them the throwing of cues and the working of whatever off-stage effects he can find time to take care of. These effects are noted in blue pencilings on margins of the play script.

The first act set represented a cliff, steps leading from the summit. The grandame of the story made her entrance over this cliff and down the steps, leaning upon one of those long staffs without which no stage grandame is complete. Opposite her entrance cue was the notation: "Taps heard off stage." Taps to a stage manager usually imply the coconut shells with which everything from a lone horseman to a cavalry charge is simulated. In this case it seemed to indicate the impact of the grandame's staff on the cliff. Why she could not do her own tapping I did not know, neither did I inquire. Stage managers all are presumed to be messengers to Garcia.

When Morrison called a scenery rehearsal I added a stick to my other properties and, as the grandame's entrance approached, tapped rhythmically on the stage floor. Morrison, who was sitting well to the rear of the house, interrupted the rehearsal and called out:

"Hey, Lloyd! Where are your taps?"

I thrust my head out of the wings and said, "I gave them, sir."

"Louder! Can't hear it back here," commanded the director.

I seized a stout club and raised the dust of many years out of the stage-floor cracks with wallops that would have done for the ominous footsteps of Dunsany's Gods of the Mountain.

In the midst of this racket Morrison's voice demanded irritably, "Lloyd, where the devil's your taps?"

Popping out of the wings, I gave the stage floor a pile-driving sock that expressed my temper and called, "Can you hear that, sir?"

Morrison eyed me and the bludgeon disgustedly. "Somebody wake up that cornetist, please, and have him blow taps," he said with crushing disdain. He did not laugh; the rest of the company attended to that detail for him, and for the balance of the engagement I was addressed exclusively as Taps.

The Bird Cage ran only briefly, and when it closed the last theater door in San Diego closed with it. I couldn't sit in my roof tent and wait for fall. Los Angeles, a much larger city, was a hundred and twenty miles away, dad was there, the theaters there did not shut down in summer and there were picture companies knocking about. If I couldn't find work on the Los Angeles stage, perhaps I could piece out the summer as an extra to this poor relation of the stage and eat until the San Diego season should revive. So I went to Los Angeles.

Assorted adventures
of Harold Lloyd:
another pot-pourri from
his films.

(1) At a train station.

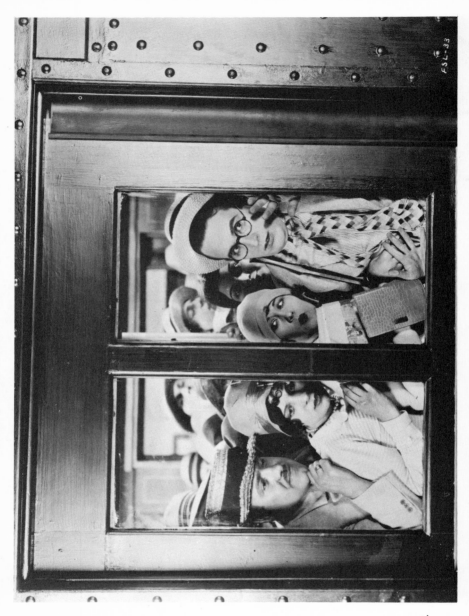

(2) In the subway.

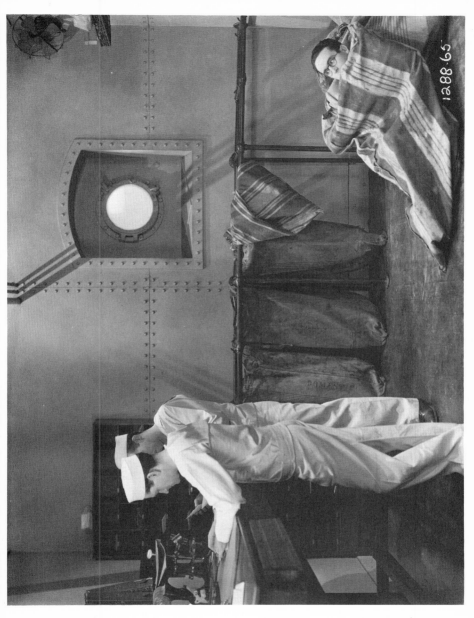

(3) On shipboard.

(4) With Mildred Davis.

(5) With Mildred Davis and a third party.

(6) At a dance.

(7) On a trolley.

(8) A typical Lloyd
predicament: hand
caught in a vase.

III

Bumps and Brodies

"ONCE upon a time there was an enchanted city called Los Angeles," is the way this chapter should begin, for in it, under other names, you will find Aladdin, Cinderella, Jack of the Beanstalk, Little Red Riding-hood, the Sleeping Princess and the poor woodcutter, not to mention the wolf, the giant, the wicked stepmother, the elder sisters, Bluebeard and Big Claus and Little Claus, producers.

A fancy paragraph and open to suspicion of real estate to sell, but an honest heart beats beneath its embroidered waistcoat. It means only that a lot can happen in fifteen years' time in Los Angeles—and has. Bagdad? A mill town with the magic-carpet works shut down.

When I came up from San Diego in the spring of 1913, my father, who was working part time in a shoe store, and I moved into the Belmont, a theatrical hotel on Main Street next to the Hippodrome, a big ten-and-fifteen-cent vaudeville house. Gaylord, who had been homesteading to discouraging results in Wyoming, joined us and became the Belmont's night clerk, while I was bell boy and relief clerk when not making the rounds of the stock companies or bucking the movie extra lines.

The Belmont was populated by small-time vaudeville and stock-burlesque people who bragged or played cards or combined the two hour upon hour in the one public room. Once a Hawaiian band stayed a week. I had been passionately fond of the sob of the steel guitar until then; since, I have gone about slitting the throats of ukuleles and I believe every word of Doctor Rockwell's learned account of the origins of Hawaiian music.

It seems, explains the doctor, that an edict once was issued in Hawaii in the time of the cruel King Kamehameha calling for the death of every male pineapple. Only one escaped. To disguise her man child from the king's ruffians, one loving mamma pineapple pulled the little fellow's whiskers out one by one, and the moaning of the boy pineapple has been preserved in "Aloha Oe" and other native airs.

There was a moment in the early Los Angeles days when I considered turning chorus man. *The Tik Tok Man of Oz* was in rehearsal and I looked on for two days, hesitating, then tightened my belt a notch and moved on. I played with the Morosco Stock Company in three bills in small parts, one of them a member of the student corps in *Old Heidelberg,* parent of the musical *Student Prince.* The wages for such parts never were more than twenty-five dollars a week, that including a week's rehearsal without pay. For one bill that survived only a week I rehearsed two weeks, making my pay $8.33 a week.

It was an extraordinary stock company—the best I ever knew. There were six in the company whom Mr. Morosco paid $100 a week each, then a good figure for a leading man, and three that drew $300 each, a great sum in 1913. Among the cast were Florence Reed, William Desmond, Thomas MacLarnie, Malcom Williams, Charles Ruggles, Harrison Hunter and Howard Scott, each of them a name. But the better the company, the less opportunity for a youngster.

So I called up the Edison people at Balboa, with whom I had worked that one day in San Diego. Yes, they were using some people; come on down. I worked with them at three dollars a day on such days as extras were needed until the company returned to New York in midsummer. In one picture I had a small bit in a barn-dance scene. When the film was shown at a Main Street ten-cent house owned by Gore Brothers, who rose later to proprietorship of the great West Coast chain of theaters, I saw myself on the screen for the first time. Vanity never took a worse wallop. The shock that comes with the first glance at the proofs the photographer mails you after the sitting is something like it. None of us photographs as he imagines himself, and, of the two likenesses, the camera's is not the flattering one. It is not altogether a matter of pulchritude, at that; you simply do not look like the self you know, and, in the case of an extra in a film bit, your part comes out at the small end of the glass.

Disgusted as I was with the movies, nothing else offered. Universal was at its original California lot at Sunset Boulevard and Gower Street, Hollywood, where the Christie studio is now, and there I went. The lot was the birthplace of pictures in Hollywood. In October of 1911 David and William Horsley, of the old Nestor company, had set out from New Jersey to join the movement Selig, Bison and Biograph had led to the coast. On the train they met a Hollywood booster—perhaps the ancestor of them all. Hollywood, a place of 5000, had been annexed to Los Angeles the year before. Land there was much cheaper than in the city proper, the booster told the Horsley brothers, while every other advantage obtained. So persuaded were the Horsleys that they went direct from the Los Angeles station to Hollywood and, without looking further, leased the old Blondeau tavern and stable at Gower and Sunset. In May, 1912, Universal had bought the studio.

Those who never have been to Southern California—and a few remain—cannot understand and are curious, I find, about the distinction between Hollywood and Los Angeles. Hollywood lies in the Cahuenga Valley, which stretches twenty miles from the original pueblo of Los Angeles to the sea at Santa Monica. Originally most of it was a cactus thicket given over to cattle and sheep. A great drought in 1879, if you will pardon a moment of drought, ruined the cattle trade and led to the first experiments with citrus trees and Chinese truck gardeners. In 1883 Horace H. Wilcox came out from Topeka, Kansas, where he had made money in real estate, and bought an apricot and fig orchard at Hollywood and Cahuenga Boulevards, now the heart of the town, as a country home. His wife named the place Hollywood, after an estate of a friend in the East.

In the midst of Los Angeles' wildest boom in 1887 Wilcox platted the estate, but sold few lots and died land poor in 1893. When the town was incorporated in 1903 its population was only 700 and one of its first ordinances prohibited the driving of sheep in flocks of more than 2000 through the streets. Seven years later, unable to command its own water supply, it succumbed to Los Angeles. By now the Cahuenga Valley is built up almost continuously to the sea. When I first knocked on the Universal's gates in 1913, Los Angeles was a city of 500,000 and there still was a reach of open country between the city and the studio; from Hollywood to the sea, a long gap, there was only the village of Sawtelle.

Four companies were working on the Universal lot. For extras there was a casting window and a bull pen with benches where you sat all day unless you could get through the gates and dog the heels of an assistant director. If you want a perfect picture of it I refer you to *Merton of the Movies*. That is a story I read and a play and picture I saw with more emotions than the author. It will be a great surprise to Harry Leon Wilson, no doubt, but I was Merton—or one of many Mertons.

The gatekeeper was a crabby old soul who let me understand that it would be a pleasure to keep me out. As I lurked about I noticed that at noon a crowd of actors and extras drifted out in make-up to eat at a lunch counter across the way, passing the gatekeeper without question each way. The next morning I brought a make-up box. At noon I dodged behind a billboard, made up, mingled with the lunch-counter press and returned with them through the gate without challenge. Once inside, I was assumed to be an extra on the job. I got no work—hardly expected to get it—but I did learn useful things about studio routine, meet older heads among the extras, learn the names of directors and assistant directors and after a time begin to register on their memories as a regular. On the way out I made a point to speak to the gateman, and on future entrances, if he looked the least suspicious I would say, carelessly, "With Smalley"— Philip Smalley being one of the directors.

Other than the leads there were four grades of picture actors. The highest made up the stock company—that is, supporting players regularly employed. Next below ranked the guaranty people—extras at the regular three dollars a day, but assured of a minimum of four or five days' work a week and given group dressing rooms. Just extras, my own classification, formed the third group, cooling their heels from eight until mid-afternoon in the bull pen. No casting window ever admitted until late in the day that no work was in prospect—a device that cost the studio nothing and assured a supply of extras if a director suddenly called for them. At two or three o'clock, when it was too late to try other studios, the word was passed from the window: "Nothing to-day, folks; but be sure to be here in the morning." Below us were only the mob extras, recruited when needed by want ads and paid one dollar a day, luncheon and car fare. They were almost exclusively hobos and an unfragrant lot, pictures not yet having attracted the curiosity seekers.

The ruse of slipping through the gates in make-up with the returning lunchers had the disadvantage of not being workable until midday, by which time all parts would have been given out. Once acquainted with the guaranty actors, however, they let me in through a window of their dressing room before the cameras started the morning grind, and I began to get work.

The masters of our destinies were the assistant directors. The director himself had too much on his mind to bother casting more than the leads. The minor and background rôles were filled by his assistant, and, if it was necessary to call upon the casting window for more extras, it was he who entered the bull pen and weeded out the waiters. Like second lieutenants, assistant directors were apt to be young and top-heavy with new authority; and, though I escaped the bull pen early, more than one assistant director wiped his shoes upon my self-respect. My armor was pasteboard and my wounds were many.

There was one very doggy director who now would be a broken old man sweeping my studio steps and tipping his hat gratefully as I rolled by in splendor if one dream had come true. The trouble about these revenge visions is that, when the day of atonement comes around, the bitter hate that sped the day has turned funny on you and the injury has revenged itself. No one ever climbed in Hollywood, I suppose, without having endless old scores to pay, and few have been small enough to pay them.

Six months or so of this, and Universal opened a large new studio across the street, turning the old lot over to small comedy companies. By this time I was more or less attached to J. Farrell Macdonald, who was directing J. Warren Kerrigan; extras who got on regularly usually were identified with one director. Kerrigan recently had come to Universal from the Flying A at Santa Barbara at the published salary of $300 a week, a figure which they could tell to the Marines as far as we extras were concerned. There wasn't that much money anywhere outside a press agent's mind, or so we thought. In Macdonald's unit I worked up from three dollars a day occasionally to five dollars and five days' work guaranteed, and picked up a character bit now and then.

Among the guaranty group was an extra who seemed to have

first call on such bits. He was a good type, but a bad actor. Macdonald and his staff would struggle with him patiently while the rest of us stood by and bit our nails, half in envy, half in agony at the man's awkwardness. Just to convince myself that the bit was child's play, I would slip behind a set and rehearse it with myself, then come back and grit my teeth.

Another teeth-gritting extra was a young fellow named Hal Roach. Born in Elmira, New York, Roach had gone to the Pacific Northwest and Alaska, then drifted down the coast and got on at the Universal ranch in the San Fernando Valley as a cowboy in Kerrigan Westerns by virtue of being able to stick on a horse. Kerrigan liked him, and when the star returned to the studio he brought Roach along.

Roach and I were cast as two thugs in one Kerrigan picture and the one small piece of business between us was given to him. Failing to satisfy the director after several tries, the business was transferred to me and I did it satisfactorily, as anyone of some stage experience could not have failed to do. Roach, who had held experience lightly, as the inexperienced do, was mildly impressed—more so when George Perilot, Macdonald's character man and a veteran actor, said some nice things about me. Perilot and I had talked make-up and he had found that I knew a trick or two not in his repertoire.

The crest of the Universal experience came with *Samson and Delilah,* a pretentious four-reel effort of Macdonald's, out of which I drew eight or nine straight five-dollar pay checks—an unusual break. A drove of mob extras were used in the picture and another guaranty man and I were told to make them up in a hurry as hairy Philistines. He took the gum arabic, I the crêpe hair, and we trotted the hobos past us on a conveyor-belt system later adopted by Henry Ford. He slapped on the gum with one motion, I a hank of hair with another, and where the hair landed it remained. Our aim was poor, but good enough for mobs in 1913.

The new studio had not been in use long when the casting routine was changed and a man named Datig made casting director. Assistant directors no longer chose their extras in the bull pen, but referred their needs to Datig. A new rule went into effect simultaneously—five dollars a day would be paid only for small parts, and extras not so employed would revert to three dollars without exception. That meant that we would earn three dollars much more often than five, and seven of us struck; rather, we refused to take three-dollar jobs, and the company retaliated by offering us nothing but three-dollar jobs so long as we held out. Moreover, stock and guaranty actors were given passes without which it was impossible to get beyond the bull pen. Some of the strikers surrendered after a few days; Roach and I never did. When I had hung about for two weeks without being offered a part and five dollars, I gave up and went to San Diego to ask Connor's advice. He told me that Allan Dwan, another director at U., once had been a pupil of his, and gave me a note to Dwan saying that I was a very capable boy and the rest of it. Dwan was very pleasant, but he had his own clan and a letter got me no further than a letter does to-day in Hollywood.

Deciding that something more was needed than my own word or some one else's that I was a useful actor, I had eight or ten photographs taken in widely varied character make-ups—the cream, in-fact, of the Lloyd Portrait Gallery. All extras made great claims for themselves, and, as the only test of these pretensions was the camera, casting directors did much of their hiring on an eenie-meenie-minie-moe basis. In such a market a sample case should have been useful, but my album was not particularly so. When Christy Cabanne, then and now a director, told me one day when I asked him for work that I was not a picture type, I flashed the album on him. Cabanne registered surprise and observed that he had been mistaken, no doubt, but he did not carry this apology to the extremity of giving me a job.

I got one finally with a small company making L. Frank Baum's Wizard of Oz stories. Following up the great success of the original story as a children's book and as a musical show with Dave Montgomery and Fred Stone as the Tin Man and Scarecrow, respectively, Baum wrote a shelf of sequels. A man named Gottschalk had the picture rights to all. I found Roach working here and he and I clowned as Hottentots and similar savages in breechclouts and bolomania, a heavy but easily removed body paint.

Roach surprised me—though "surprise" is a faint word for it—one day by announcing that he had got hold of several thousand dollars with which he intended making pictures on his own. He would be the director and I could be the first brick in his company at the usual three dollars a day. A few days later he rented a corner in the Bradbury mansion as an office, with the use of a stage in the back yard, and Hal Roach was a producer.

The big Bradbury house stands atop the abrupt Court Street Hill, looking down on downtown Los Angeles, and is just about the best surviving example in the city of pre-stucco California architecture. It is a place of many turrets, bay windows, wood carvings and curlicues, a grand staircase, sixteen-foot ceilings, brocaded wall papers, stained glass, parqueted floors, hardwood finish, sliding doors and all the other elegancies of the 80's. In the yard a giant palm soars 110 feet and a rubber tree has grown so huge now that its roots are pushing up the cement walks. We called it Pneumonia Hall, from its wide and windy spaces. John Bradbury, a pioneer, built it, but the family had not lived there in some years. Mary Pickford, Chaplin, Hobart Bosworth, Max Figman and lesser actors had made pictures there, and two or three small companies were officed and working there when Roach rented his cubby-hole. There was not another building in Los Angeles so combining location and magnificence. The grand staircase was photographed so much that it still is a little up-stage to-day, when the upper floors have become an old folks' home and the superior court judges use the first floor as a luncheon club and the old stable as a garage.

Roach had an idea that there would be novelty and money in kid pictures—a conviction which he vindicated eventually with the *Our Gang* comedies. He hired two boys and built his first picture, a one-reel comedy, around their boisterous day at the beach. I was the adult lead—the chauffeur who chaperoned them and bore the brunt of their boyish mischief, the little dears. Soon after, Jane Novak joined us and Roach made a straight comedy in which she and I played the leads. Next he picked up an eccentric comedian and made four pictures with him. These being even worse than the previous two, the eccentric departed and Roach said:

"Harold, you've got to be the low comedian. Think up some funny get-up and let's get busy."

Another one-reeler followed in which I ad-libbed old comedy gags from the opening shot to the last. To ad-lib is to improvise, to make up as you go along, but neither definition quite preserves the flavor.

Roach exclaimed, with unflattering surprise, "Hell! You're a comedian! I'll pay you five dollars. Now think up a character for yourself and we will be set."

I experimented with dress and make-up and about the fifth picture settled on a character we christened Willie Work. The name wrongly suggests a tramp; it was, instead, a hash of different low-comedy get-ups, with a much-padded coat, a battered silk hat and a cat's-whisker mustache as its distinguishing marks.

A counterbalance device called the Court Flight hauls passengers up and down the short steep grade of Court Street Hill at a penny fare, one car descending on a cable as the other ascends. One of Roach's early inspirations was to have Willie Work roll down this flight between the two tracks. The cameraman stationed himself at the bottom and pointed his lens up the flight. When I had rolled down, with many bruises, and the film was developed Willie Work was found, inexplicably, to be rolling on a level roadway. We were so green at the business that we did not know that if you want angle in a picture you first must get angle in your lens. By inclining his camera at the same gradient as that of my descent, the cameraman had flattened it out to a spirit-level smoothness.

Roach put arnica on my bruises and sirup on my vanity and we tried it a second time. Now the cameraman stationed himself in a second-story window across Spring Street at the foot of the flight. His angle was true, but there is more than one dimension to a picture; the scene had been taken at such a distance that Willie Work was a mere blob on the developed negative. We might as well have rolled a dummy down the incline. There was no third time.

In another Willie Work picture Roach thought up the droll idea of putting me to bed with a skunk. The polecat's first line of defense had been removed and Roach told me that he had read somewhere that a skunk so treated makes a perfect pet, as playful, affectionate and gentle as a kitten. Evidently the skunk had not read the article, for he bit me, and not in affection.

Nor was Hal's optimism confined to skunks. Different friends would drop in and watch our daily rushes. If permitted they escaped without comment, but if cornered they usually said,

"Well, to tell the truth, Hal, it's pretty terrible."

As regularly as they said it Roach replied, "We don't care; we like it."

When a picture was finished it was expressed to New York to a distributor. The speed with which the films bounded back to us could be explained only on the theory that the distributors hired some one in Chicago to meet the trains there and turn them around. None ever was sold and all presumably have been burned long ago to recover the metallic silver. A new independent producer sells his product where and if he can for whatever he can get, and vaults in Los Angeles and New York are stuffed with hundreds of films that never found a market— a dead loss to their makers. The independent's goal is not to sell a film here and there, but to capture a contract from a distributor to produce a specific line or type of picture, the distributor financing production in part and sharing its risks in return for exclusive rights and the larger share of the profits.

Roach must have been scraping the bottom of the barrel by the time we made a picture called *Just Nuts.* For it he employed Roy Stewart, a well-known heavy in Westerns, as leading man. Jane Novak was leading woman, I the comedian. We put a gag in every scene and made a funny film, as funny films went then. Pathé liked it so well that they not only bought it but offered a contract to Roach if he could sign up his three leads.

A program was mapped out calling for a one-reel comedy one week and a two-reel drama the next, Stewart to play the leads in the dramas and I the second business—sometimes as many as three parts. In the comedies I was to have the lead. Then came the discovery that Stewart was getting ten dollars a day. The following exchange of verbal notes took place between Roach and Lloyd:

> *Lloyd:* How come you are paying Stewart ten dollars and me only five?
> *Roach:* Well, Harold, you see, it is this way: Stewart won't work for less than ten dollars and I simply can't pay two men that much. Now if you will be patient and wait until we are on our feet—
> *Lloyd:* As I understand it, Stewart is getting ten dollars because he asked for it. If that is the way to get ten dollars I ask for it too.

Roach: I'm sorry. You know that I'd like to pay you ten
dollars and more if I could, but we can't afford it.

Lloyd: I'm sorry, too, and I guess that I shall have to try to
get it somewhere else.

Roach: Well, good luck, Harold.

Lloyd: So long, Hal.

Roach hired Dick Rossin in my place. After three pictures
the enterprise foundered and Roach went to Essanay as a director. Meanwhile I was marking time at the Keystone lot in
Edendale, where for three weeks they kept mè dangling on
promises.

"Yes, sir, Lloyd, we are going to give you this and that," they
told me daily—and gave me nothing.

As I was on the point of looking elsewhere, they tried me out
as an Italian fruit-cart vender. I surprised the director with an
unexpectedly good make-up, but he was only mildly interested
in whether I looked like an Italian pedler or a Norwegian
fisherman. The action called for a motorcycle to rip through
my fruit cart and for me to take a comedy fall in the midst of
the fruit. Could I fall or was I just an upright actor was the
question. Keystone comedies were a series of falls and Keystoners
fell as no one has since Adam and Niagara.

The cart was a breakaway, built in two sections. It burst
asunder as the motorcycle charged through, the fruit erupted
and I leaped into the air and came down on the back of my neck
among oranges and bananas to the critical approval of the
director. I was one of them. Such a fall is called, for no reason
at all, a 108. In its usual form it begins with a flying brick, the
brick hits the artist in the head, he leaps up, turns a semi-flip-
flap and lands on the peak of his spine. In the field of 108's Ben
Turpin knew no peer. When called upon at benefits, his contribution invariably was, without introduction or peroration,
a series of grim and cross-eyed kerflops on his neck.

There are tricks of muscular relaxation in all stage falls, of
course, but by the end of a Keystone day the most accomplished
faller wished for goofer feathers. Bumps and Brodies, the latter
after the gifted Steve who said he jumped from the Brooklyn
Bridge, are other studio names for falls in general, and the
artist is a bumper. Bobbie Dunn was doing a scene with a girl
in a Ford Sterling picture at Edendale one day. The scene went

so well that Sterling wished to keep it going beyond the rehearsed action. He shouted to Dunn, "Ad-lib, Bobbie, ad-lib!" Bobbie dropped his girl partner, went into a series of Brodies and accepted the shrieks that followed as a spontaneous tribute to his artistry.

Sterling had been the Number 1 Comedian of the business, pressed, then passed by Chaplin by then. He knew what he wanted to the point of being finicky, spoke his mind freely and had the reputation of being a hard man to work for. When I got through my first picture with him with only one rebuke and talked him out of that one, it was studio gossip that I was carrying a rabbit's foot. The scene was a jail break. I looked back, saw the guards coming and ran. Sterling wanted me to do a comic Sterling jump here. When he did it, it was funny, but I argued that it was not natural to a straight character and won him around.

Once or twice I worked with Fatty Arbuckle, but with little success. Arbuckle had the star bumpers of the lot and he led them in person, taking Brodies that shook buildings. I could bump with any of them, but he surrounded himself with a group of regulars who knew his methods so well that they did not need to be told what to do, and weren't, leaving a new man to guess and flounder. The vogue of the Keystone cops was waning, and, though they still were being used occasionally, I never happened to be cast as one.

Roach was dickering with Pathé again. They renewed their offer of a contract if he could engage Roy Stewart, Jane Novak and me, but Stewart and Novak were signed up elsewhere and Hal had to wire New York that only his comedian was available. After a little delay, Pathé replied instructing him to go ahead with me. Roach offered me fifty dollars a week, with a promise of more as soon as and if the pictures were successful.

During the making of my last picture at Keystone I sat alongside Sterling on a log on location one afternoon.

"Well, I'm leaving after this picture," I told him. "Roach is starting up again and he is going to give me fifty a week."

"You're foolish to bother with that stuff," Sterling said. "You never will get anywhere in cheap comedies. I think you can act. If you want my advice, get in with D. W. Griffith and do the Bobbie Harron sort of thing. There's a future there and Griffith can make you."

From where Sterling sat, the advice was sound. He knew me only as a juvenile, for I had played perfectly straight and sympathetic juvenile leads for him. On the other hand, he knew that the Roach comedies had been pretty sad.

"No more minnow in the pond for me," I objected. "At Roach's I can be the big fish in the puddle."

Hampton del Ruth, business manager for Mack Sennett, said he was sorry to see me go.

"We like your work and you have a better future with Keystone than with some shoestring outfit. In fact we were just about to give you a graduated contract."

All of which was news to me—the sort of news you never hear until you leave. I told him that I had given my word to Roach.

"Anyway, I believe I am doing the wiser thing," I added. "You have Conklin, Arbuckle, Sterling and other good comedians and I would be a long time getting anywhere against that competition. Why pick out the highest wall to jump when there are plenty of curbstones around?"

"How about a new character?" Roach asked when we were back at the Bradbury mansion.

Chaplin was going great guns, his success such that unless you wore funny clothes and otherwise aped him you were not a comedian. Exhibitors who could not get the original demanded imitations—and were given them in numbers from brazen counterfeits to coy skirtings about the Chaplin manner. Had I had the glass character then, and had I been allowed to try it out, I have no doubt that it would have sold on its merits, but these are two large ifs. On the one hand, I had only vague yearnings to do something different; on the other, the distributors and exhibitors would hear of no departures from the Chaplin track.

I told Roach that I had something that was an improvement on Willie Work, at least. When he saw it he approved. Later it was tagged with the name of Lonesome Luke. For it my father had found a worn pair of Number 12AA last shoes in a repair shop on Los Angeles Street, where they had been left for resoling by an Englishman on his uppers. Dad asked the cobbler if he thought five dollars would compensate the owner. The cobbler was sure of it—five dollars bought a good pair of shoes. In a haberdashery dad found a black-and-white vertical-striped shirt and bought out the stock. The coat of a woman's tailored suit, a pair of very tight and short trousers, a vest too short, a cut-down collar, a cut-down hat and two dots of a mustache completed the original version of Lonesome Luke. The cunning thought behind all this, you will observe, was to reverse the Chaplin outfit. All his clothes were too large, mine all too small. My shoes were funny, but different; my mustache funny, but different.

Nevertheless, the idea was purely imitative and was recognized as such by audiences, though I painstakingly avoided copying the well-known Chaplin mannerisms.

On location one day a boy called to me, "Say, we had a contest at our theater last week and you beat Sterling." For just an instant I was flattered, then I realized that he had taken me for Chaplin.

If I dropped into a theater to study the audience's response to a Lonesome Luke film, I took a chance on hearing a childish voice pipe in the darkness, "Oh, mamma, see the funny man, Charlie Chaplin," or a hard-boiled boy critic growl, "Aw, I know him; he ain't Charlie."

Not only was the get-up imitative but it was an offense to the eye originally. I cleaned it up as time went on until it was self-respecting before it died, but I do not like to recall it and I am sorry that it is necessary to exhume it for this autopsy.

To our pain and puzzlement, Pathé sent us four scenarios by Tad Dorgan, the sports cartoonist, to begin on and made their use part of the contract. We never had worked from a scenario. We never had heard of a comedy being made from a scenario, unless it was *Tillie's Punctured Romance*. I am not sure that we ever had seen a scenario.

The earliest method of comedy construction was to begin with a policeman or policemen to chase your comedian. The rest of the cast was optional, except that there must be a girl. Westlake Park and Echo Park, where Aimee McPherson's Angelus Temple now stands, were convenient and free to all comers; likewise the sunlight, and the remainder was up to your ingenuity.

The product was as careless as the method and the first technical advance was to decide first on two gags, then build one reel of film around them. The rest was stuffing, but two gags were held to be ample to carry a comedy, until Chaplin, in reckless disregard of the conservation of natural resources, began to load his pictures with gags. The competition deplored this as un-sporting and non-union, but hurried after him.

The third method, and the one we used when we had disposed of the Tad scenarios, was to begin with a locale.

"We will make this a shoe-string picture," Roach would decree, for example; or it might be a Chinese laundry, a hotel, roller-skating rink, delicatessen shop, Jewish tailor shop, restaurant, amusement park or what you will. The locale suggested the comedy and as we went along we thought up enough story to string it on.

The chief objection to a scenario was that it was written with-out regard to our limitations. Tad was a New York newspaper-man, concerned only with laying out the front elevation of a funny story. He did not know or care that the company in Los Angeles which would make the story was restricted to $1200 ex-pense and a week's time. That was the buyer's lookout. The buyer was Pathé. They bought to insure better stories, but with little more understanding than Tad of our difficulties.

When we had made the four scenarios as well as we could, and Pathé had seen the product, they understood our problem better and sent us no more. They were our first and last; to this day we never use a scenario. By the time their use was feasible we were so accustomed to shooting without a script that we go on doing it in six to eight reels as we did in one. It has its disadvantages in time and money, and regularly we say, when a picture is finished, that the next will be shot from a script. Perhaps the next one will.

Believe it or not, there was a time in Los Angeles when it was necessary to fare forth in search of feminine beauty and talent. The first of the Tad four was a bloomer-girl baseball story. We lacked a leading woman and the wages paid did not attract a long line of applicants. It used to be a custom with many Los Angeles apartment houses to fit up their basements with pianos and dance floors and to give weekly and semi-weekly dances to attract and hold young people. I liked to dance, did so often at these free parties, and knew that there was no lack of pretty girls in the city. I suggested to Roach that we might find a leading woman at such a dance, and we did—a pretty blonde. She left after the first picture, other experiments followed, and about the

sixth picture Bebe Daniels came and remained, to mutual satisfaction. Bebe was a dark, dewy, big-eyed child of only fifteen or
sixteen, but she came of a theatrical family and had been a stage
child.

Harry—Snub—Pollard joined the company about the same
time, Roach wanting a foil for me. Pollard was a relict of an
Australian vaudeville act, Pollard's Lilliputians. The troupe
broke up over here and most of its members took the name Pollard professionally as they went their separate ways. It was a
law of comedy that every comedian must have a comic mustache
—or "mo," as the trade name goes—and that it must be distinc-
tive. Chester Conklin had a walrus effect, Chaplin a toothbrush,
and the field was pretty well preëmpted. We went to a wig
maker's in search of a new effect for Pollard, and after much
looking he accidentally reversed a pair of Kaiser Wilhelm mus-
tachios in trying them on. The result was so absurd and original
that we looked no further and they have been Pollard's trade-
mark ever since.

Make-up and lighting experiments were creeping in as directors
and cameramen grew more expert. A new cameraman, joining
us from a dramatic company, brought with him a yellow make-
up which was in use there. Much against our will, Pollard and I
were forced to adopt it. We did not know why we disliked it,
but we found a convincing reason later. The yellow produced
uniformity and thereby made the cameraman's work easier. When
we saw the developed film it was apparent that uniformity was
not an asset to a comedy; the comedian needed contrast. Roach
agreeing with us, Snub and I carried the yellow make-up to the
back fence, counted 1-2-3 and threw it as far as we could.

Our first experiments with electric lighting were at Court Street.
We covered the diffuser frame with tarpaulin, shutting out the
direct sunlight, and turned on the carbon arcs. The scene, a
country-hotel set, was underlighted and the results poor, including an epidemic of Klieg eyes. Never having heard of Klieg eyes,
we did not know what plague had visited us. The sensation is
that of a cinder in the eye, magnified many times. Thereafter we
wore dark glasses except when before the camera.

In 1915 we had to move from Court Street for some forgotten
reason and Roach rented the old Norbig studio, half a block from
Keystone. From Norbig we moved to Santa Monica Boulevard,

Make-up character studies
from the album Harold
carried with him to Hollywood
in search of a job.

Lonesome Luke; as the fans
remember him best, and in
his final dressy stage.

The Rolin Company gathered in Westlake Park for the second Lonesome Luke one-reeler. Harold with the cane.

The first phase of Lloyd's "glass character," 1919.

then back to Court Street. All this while we were making one-reel Lonesome Lukes that were released to exhibitors at about twenty-five dollars a week rental as program fillers.

If you do not remember them and cannot imagine them, they best can be described for you by quoting the trade papers of 1915-16. A Pathé advertisement in one in the fall of 1915 calls me the Human Rubber Ball. Another ad of about that time carries a photograph of Bebe, Snub and me under the caption: "Getting Ready for the Rough Stuff in a Rolin Single Reeler—and They Can Do It." A trade-paper reviewer, writing of a new one-reeler, exclaims:

> Harold Lloyd must be made of India rubber. The way he suffers himself to be kicked all over the map, hit on the head with a mallet and fall down a dizzy flight of stairs is marvelous.

In the scrapbook, among these trade-paper clippings, I find a booklet issued by Pathé under date of January 1, 1916. A page is given to *Lonesome Luke* and another comedy feature, but the players in both are anonymous. The named stars, each given a page and a photograph, are Ruth Roland, Pearl White, Lolita Robertson, Jackie Saunders, Fania Marinoff, Jeanne Eagels, Lois Meredith, Florence Reed, Lillian Lorraine, Kathryn Browne-Decker, Margaret Green, José Collins and Bliss Milford.

How many names do you recognize? How many survive in pictures? Jeanne Eagels was co-starred with Jack Gilbert in a Monta Bell picture in 1927 and the critics all spoke of it as her film debut. They did not know or had forgotten that she was featured in pictures years before she made her great stage success in *Rain*. Excepting Miss Eagels, who is a returned prodigal, none is acting before the camera to-day to my knowledge and two or three are blanks in my memory.

Ruth Roland put her earnings as a serial queen into real estate and is reputed to be the wealthiest woman in Los Angeles to-day, but she is retired. Pearl White was in France the last I heard. Florence Reed and Fania Marinoff have returned to the stage. José Collins, daughter of Lottie Collins, now is Lady Robert Innes-Ker, wife of a brother of the Duke of Roxburghe, and lives in England. The late Frank Curzon, British producer, left her an income of $100,000 in his will. I have no idea what has become of some of the others. The mortality rate in Hollywood is as high as it used to be in Panama in yellow-fever days.

We went to San Diego during the 1915 exposition, seeking new backgrounds, and took three pictures, one at the exposition, another at the Tia Juana race track; a third was a warship story. The Navy lent us the use of a battleship deck and were cordial hosts. Bebe may have had something to do with that. One morning the executive officer asked Roach if he and his troupe would give the officers the pleasure of their company at luncheon in, the ward room. Roach accepted, then took us aside, warned us to be gentlemen and reflect honor upon the infant industry, and added a few pointers on table etiquette until we were well cowed.

The entrée was a planked steak or fish with an ornamental border of potatoes. None of us, Roach included, ever had met up with a planked dish, nor were we conversant with potatoes in their ornamental moods. In fact, we were not at all sure that they were potatoes. The first man served removed a slice of meat and left the ornamental border severely alone. The rest of us took our cue from him. Then a second plank was set before the executive officer, who scooped a tablespoon into the molding as if it had been so much food, as we began to suspect that it might be, and his brother officers laid vandal hands upon the rest of it. Personally I looked for mutiny to break out in the cook's galley any minute, but nothing happened. Well, you know how it is. By unspoken agreement we all pretended to be on a violently antipotato diet. When the dessert arrived it was seen to be a handsome shortcake. We boarded it like so many hijackers, resolved to make up that potato deficiency, and left no scrap of it. Then no second shortcake arrived for the officers; there was only one—and Roach's mouth was stopped with guilty cake.

When we returned to Court Street from Santa Monica Boulevard we began making Lonesome Luke in two reels in answer to exhibitor demand, giving two weeks instead of one to each. Roach is a born leader, an excellent business man and an original comedy director, but he was not so happy at the new two-reel length. When he had worked a week on one he had a way of asking, "How much footage have we now?" The answer would be 1400 feet or thereabout, whereupon Hal would call "Well, boys, let's finish her up," and shoot the remainder as if he had a train to catch. No matter what went before, the slighted final 400 feet would let the picture down with a soggy thud. It brought my discontent with Lonesome Luke to a head.

I was convinced both that the character had gone as far as we could take him and that I had a better. The hazy idea in the back of my head was crystallizing. I had been feeling around for youth, possibly a boy who could be carried through a college series, a comedy Frank Merriwell, for a long time, when I saw a dramatic picture at a downtown theater while we still were at Norbig. The central character was a fighting parson, tolerant and peaceful until riled, then a tartar. Glasses emphasized his placidity. The heavy had stolen the girl, carrying her away on horseback. The parson leaped on another horse, pursued, overtook the villain, dragged him from his horse and the two were lost in a cloud of dust. When the dust cleared, the heavy lay prone and still, while the parson dusted his clothes with careless flecks of his handkerchief, replaced his glasses and resumed his ministerial calm.

I did not feel cut out for a fighting parson, but the basic idea was there. A picture actor named Mortenson, who lived in the same apartment house on Fourth Street just off Hill, and I talked over its comedy possibilities night after night. The glasses would serve as my trade-mark and at the same time suggest the character—quiet, normal, boyish, clean, sympathetic, not impossible to romance. I would need no eccentric make-up, "mo" or funny clothes. I would be an average recognizable American youth and let the situations take care of the comedy. The comedy should be better for not depending upon a putty nose or its equivalent and the situations should be better for not being tied to low-comedy coat tails; funnier things happen in life to an ordinary boy than to a Lonesome Luke. Exaggeration is the breath of picture comedies, and obviously they cannot be true to life, but they can be recognizably related to life.

Probably the vision was not so clear in my mind at the time as all this; what I write now benefits by hindsight, yet I saw it clearly enough. How about Pathé, though? They could not be expected willingly to trade Lonesome Luke for a pig in a poke. By advertising, promotion and good distribution they had done their part to create a market for him and make him a comedy staple, the demand growing healthily. This new idea of mine might be anything or nothing—probably nothing; but whichever, it called for scrapping a going commodity at nothing on the dollar and starting from scratch with an unknown quantity. Had I been in New York I doubt that I could have transmitted my enthusiasm convincingly, and I was a long way from New York.

So discouraging was the prospect that I decided to give up comedy pictures and make a fresh beginning myself. After long, hard work, I was getting $100 a week, a fortune relative to my past earnings, but not so much alongside Chaplin's reputed $1000 a week. I told Roach that I was fed up on Luke, convinced that Pathé never would agree to a change and resolved to go into dramatic pictures, where I was certain I could do something. Roach was going to New York anyway. On a previous trip he had seen a clown at the Hippodrome and become enthusiastic about his picture possibilities. Now he was returning to bring him to the coast and star him in two-reel pictures.

The situation was a strain on Roach's optimism, but it was equal to it.

"It won't do any harm to put it up to Pathé, anyway," he argued. "As I see it, they are going to lose Luke whichever way the bird jumps. Unless they think you are bluffing, they are likely to take a chance on a change, and I think I can show them that you mean it."

Privately I believed that Pathé would conclude to hire another comedian and carry on with Lonesome Luke. Audiences would detect the substitution, but the picture was Luke, not Lloyd. Roach, however, argued my case better than I could have done, and won. He wired back that Pathé consented. Did I wish to make one- or two-reel pictures in the new character?

One, I decided. One-reel subjects still were popular with exhibitors as program fillers. We could make and release a picture a week; a new character needed the constant hammering of fifty-two releases a year to familiarize it. And if we made a bad one, worse luck, it would be forgotten quickly.

IV

Magic Glasses

THERE is more magic in a pair of horn-rimmed glasses than the opticians dream of, nor did I guess the half of it when I put them on in 1917.

With them, I am Harold Lloyd; without them a private citizen. I can stroll unrecognized down any street in the land at any time without the glasses, a boon granted no other picture actor and one which some of them would pay well for. At a cost of seventy-five cents they provide a trademark recognized instantly wherever pictures are shown. They make low-comedy clothes unnecessary, permit enough romantic appeal to catch the feminine eye, usually averted from comedies, and they hold me down to no particular type or range of story.

It was chance that they are horn-rimmed. The parson's glasses in the dramatic picture that inspired them were not tortoise shells, but when I came to choose a pair of my own the vogue of horn rims was new and it was youth, principally, that was adopting them. The novelty was a picture asset and the suggestion of youth fitted perfectly with the character I had in mind.

We took out the lenses immediately, knowing that the reflection of light on the glass would be troublesome, and thought we were doing a new thing. As usual, however, the Chinese did it first. Give a historian time and he will prove that Mack Sennett did not invent the Keystone cop and the bathing beauty, but that both were popular comedy pictures in Cathay in the Ming dynasty and are mentioned by Marco Polo. A correspondent wrote me from Peking recently that not only were tortoise-shell glasses worn in China as a mark of rank in the time of the Middle Kingdom, more than a thousand years ago, but that it was not uncommon to wear them without lenses. "Damned clever, these Chinese," as Bobbie Clark said.

The first pair, bought out of stock, were too heavy; the second pair had so large a diameter that the rims covered my eyebrows and killed a great deal of expression. A third pair that just suited was found in a little optical shop in Spring Street, after scouring Los Angeles. I remember hunting through a tray containing probably thirty pairs before coming on the right one. I wore them for a year and a half, guarding them with my life. When the frame broke from wear and tear I went on patching it with everything, from paste to spirit gum for three months, until progressive dissolution forced us to send them East to an optical-goods manufacturer for duplication.

The manufacturers shipped us back twenty pairs tailored to the measure of the old faithfuls and returned our check. The advertising we had given tortoise-shell rims, they wrote, still left them in our debt. Since then all our rims have been tailor-made by this firm.

With the last two-reel Lonesome Luke, begun as Roach set out for New York, J. Farrell Macdonald, who had given me my first job at Universal, came to me as director. Macdonald long since has put away his megaphone and become a featured player with Fox.

Unexpected as Pathé's agreement to the scrapping of Lonesome Luke was, Roach's wire was the signal for booting Luke down the Court Flight into oblivion and jumping into the new character at once. I had played with the idea so long that no further thought was needed. The opening picture was *Over the Fence*—like Tad's first scenario, a baseball story. Pollard and I were two tailors who clumsily snipped a coat tail off a customer's Prince Albert and found two baseball tickets in the pocket.

On a release-a-week schedule a picture had to be finished in five days, leaving two days in which to thresh out the next story —a situation similar to that of a stock company playing one bill and rehearsing the next. Roach was a shrewd comedy director. We had worked in tandem for years and I missed his expert hand, while Macdonald was lost in the crazy world of comedies. We did nothing in the way to which he was used and there was no time for him to learn by experience.

The opening picture called, on the third day, for a baseball park scene and forty extras—an extraordinary number for us in that time. Both the heavy expense and the schedule demanded that we finish at the ball park in one day. Macdonald had begun directing the story, but by the end of a trying day at the park he concluded that he had miscast himself and very gracefully bowed himself out. Oddly, he since has made a notable name for himself in portraying comedy rôles on the screen.

Inasmuch as I had written the story and devised all the gags, I was in a position to step in and finish the picture on my own. Dwight Whiting, Roach's business partner, asked me to take over the direction pending Hal's return from New York, which I did.

When Roach returned with his new star we were demoted to second fiddle and the small backstage. They took the front-stage and Hal gave all his time to the clown, leaving me to sink or swim in the new pond I had cried for. From the splashing that went on it was hard to say for a time whether it was sinking or swimming. I had to think up story and gags, direct and play the lead at the rate of a picture a week—a judgment, some might have thought, upon my willful head. I was desperate enough shortly to take on a former Keystone cop actor as director. Then Pollard suggested Alf Goulding, another former member of Pollard's Lilliputians. Goulding was hired on the theory that if he was any good at all I would alternate him with the former Keystone actor, giving each a week in which to work out his story. Goulding proved to be innocent of any camera knowledge; but, an old vaudevillian, he could pull gags out of the air, and thin air at that, and was a tremendous help. With his alternate, I had to supply the gags as well and virtually direct for the week he presided.

He left, Gilbert Pratt took his place and Goulding and Pratt alternated until, unexpectedly, Pathé canceled on the clown pictures, and, Roach being free again, returned to me. The clown was a remarkable contortionist and a wise old panto-mimist, but his style, effective on the stage, was overbroad for the screen, and, in addition, he had a minor cast in one eye. It was so inconsequential that no one noticed it until the first close-up. Close-ups distort any facial variation from the normal, and close-ups are essential to love scenes, while love scenes are pretty essential to pictures.

Now Pratt went to acting in our pictures and Roach and Goulding alternated as directors. Goulding was broader in his comedy, Hal a little more sincere and subdued, and the contrast was excellent for weekly release pictures. Moreover, the rivalry sped up production. Goulding and I often finished a picture in three days—once made a good one in a day and a half, giving Roach a mark to shoot at.

At quitting time one evening Goulding said to me, "There is no reason why you should come down before noon to-morrow; we have a lot of scenes ahead that you are not in and we can shoot them in the morning."

His words were sweet, for I had been working a coolie's hours for months, and I slept the next morning until the telephone woke me. Roach was on the wire.

"What's the matter?" he demanded. "It's nine o'clock; are you sick?" There was suspicion, not solicitude, in the query. I explained that Goulding had given me the morning off, and why. "I don't care if he doesn't need you," Roach barked. "The rest of us have to get down here at eight o'clock and we can't have you rolling in at noon. It's bad for morale."

That was the only time in a good many years' association, first as employee and employer, then as partners, that Roach and I tangled. My reply was such that he hung up the receiver with a furious bang. When I arrived at the studio—and not a second before twelve o'clock—Dwight Whiting sought me out. Roach's original partner had been Dan Linthicum and the name Rolin Comedies was a combination of their names. Whiting had followed Linthicum in the partnership.

"Roach says that either you or he has to get out," Whiting told me. "You can see where that leaves me. I don't know what it's all about, and I don't care, but I'm Roach's partner and I have to string along with him. You know I'm sorry—"

"I don't care what you do," I cut in, "so long as you pay me according to contract. Here I am, ready to work, and here I will be every morning unless you give me a written release from reporting."

Dwight did give me a release after several mornings of seeing my face at the usual time, and Roach made a school picture with Snub and Bebe. Pathé returned an unfavorable report on it and asked what had happened to his comedian. Learning, they sent a man to Los Angeles to patch up the quarrel. The official telephoned, asking me to come to his room at the Alexandria Hotel at a specified hour. He sent the same request to Roach, neglecting to tell either of us that the other dear charmer would be present. We met, glared fiercely—and ten minutes later shook hands. Each of us is mulish and independent and it needed outside intervention; we have disagreed about money since, but we never have lost our tempers.

Six months later the time arrived for my salary to jump from $150 a week to $300 a week on a graduated contract signed long before. As the day approached, Hal and Whiting called me into the office and unfolded the old hard-luck story. The terms of the contract were admitted, but the pictures were not turning a profit that admitted of such a salary, they explained. If I insisted on having my pound of flesh they would be forced to shut up shop; but, if I would just gamble with them a little longer, big things were just around the corner. To evidence their good faith they called in their accountant, Warren Doane, and had him show me the books.

They were getting about $2600 out of each one-reel glass picture, I knew, leaving them a profit, though not a large one. On the other hand, I knew that when Pathé increased the advance from $1200 to $1500, Roach had plowed it all back into the pictures. That was sound business practice; but why should they ask a salaried employee, without an interest in the business or a percentage of the picture, to share their gamble? Actually what they asked was that I give them $150 a week toward a speculation with big stakes. If they won I got my $150 a week back and they got the stakes, if they lost I lost too. I told them so.

I had done my part by giving the pictures all I had. I had looked forward to that $300 a week for three years and had been counting the days for months. I did not question their books, but, as an actor, I already owned a morocco-bound set of the World's Best Hard Luck Stories. Moreover, I had saved my money, had $3000 in the bank and would eat for a while, job or no job. So I stood by the terms of the contract. The discussion was renewed daily until the contract date, when, with both sides still holding their ground, we shook hands all around and I stepped out.

Dad had hurt his arm some time before and had become my adviser and housekeeper. We lived in a two-room-and-kitchen-ette apartment in the Delbert on Fremont Street, where he cooked for both of us—his spaghetti Italian was famous with the Roach troupe—mended my clothes and generally took care of me, and home to him I went.

This is as good a time as any to tell of dad's two appearances in pictures. The day we were taking the ball-park scene in *Over the Fence* we discovered that we had failed to provide for an umpire.

"Why not use your father?" Macdonald had suggested.

"All right, tell him to put on a good make-up," I agreed.

And did he? He was an advance showing of what the well-made-up chorus girl will wear; and when we were done admiring him we put a catcher's mask on his face and blotted out his masterpiece utterly.

His other appearance was at the studio. I was playing a youth out of work who sees a sign, "Book Agent Wanted," on a shop door, stops, tears up the sign to signify that the job is filled and breezes in. We decided that the bit would be funnier if the shop owner were to look out and see his sign destroyed by the fresh youth. There was no shopkeeper in the cast, but dad was standing by and we drafted him, Roach and I explaining exactly what we wanted of him.

Now when you call upon dad to act he acts! He shook up the part like a terrier worrying a rat and so convulsed Roach and me that we fell on each other's necks and wept tears of pure joy. Six or seven times we tried to shoot that bit, and each time at a certain point Hal and I collapsed, dad's indignation mounting until he flounced off the set and told us heatedly to play it ourselves.

He repaid this unfilial conduct by taking better care of me than ever, and I needed his moral support just now. When I looked for other work I found the studios polite and evasive. Whiting, as he told me later, had passed the word along that I was not a free agent.

"This is just a passing contract dispute," he told every one, "and Lloyd will be back at work with us any day."

Inopportunely for Roach at a moment when his featured player was striking for more money, the current one-reel glass

picture was being shown at Sid Grauman's Million Dollar
Theater and getting great notices. The original glass picture,
Over the Fence, had had its first run at the Theater de Luxe,
opposite Westlake Park, which was faster company than Lonesome Luke ever had traveled in; but now we were downtown in
the headline spot of the coast, where no Roach film ever had
been booked before. Not until a year later did I learn that the
firm had refused to let the following picture go into the Million
Dollar for fear of turning—or further turning—my head.

It began to look as if Roach held the winning cards, and at
eleven o'clock one morning in March, 1918, I decided suddenly
to go to New York, threw some clothes into a suitcase and caught
the noon train.

"I'm going to go see the Pathé people and tell them my side
of the story," I said to dad and to Gil Pratt, who had dropped in
the apartment. "Probably it will do no good, but I want them
to know that I did not run out on them, anyway."

I never had seen New York, had not been east of Chicago, had
been there only once as a child on a visit. There was no one on
the train whom I knew, and dad was not there to buck me up. I
looked out of the windows for 3000 miles and asked the landscape
if I had been a sap, and echo answered yes. Having taken the
stand, I was stubborn enough to hold to it through Hollywood
and high water, but I had my private misgivings that I was out
on the end of a limb and sawing it off behind me, which was no
conquering mood in which to storm the walls of New York for
the first time.

There must be several hundred thousand men and women
who can look back on their first descent, young and alone, on
those forbidding bastions and remember what it felt like. Well,
I was twenty-five years old, out of a job, a minor picture actor in
Los Angeles and no one in New York, and I had the same sinking
sensation that will overtake the boys and girls who will emerge
to-morrow, and to-morrow for the first time, from the Pennsylvania and the Grand Central terminals. I never have known any
one who was not overawed by New York's high hat the first time
they met it on the home grounds, and I don't believe that I care
to know one. Such self-confidence has its uses, but not in friend-
ship.

W. O. Douglas had given me a card to the Friars as I was

leaving Los Angeles, but I found the club filled and took a room at the Bristol, a small hotel near by in Forty-eighth Street. My first act—and I recommend it to all newly arrived pilgrims—was to buy two theater tickets, one for the matinée that day of *Sinbad* with Al Jolson, the other for Fred Stone's show at the Globe that night.

Any theater is home to me, and Jolson so rallied my morale that, when coming out of the theatre I noticed that it was just after five o'clock, I boldly called the Pathé offices and asked for Paul Brunet, who had just been made general manager.

"Mr. Brunet has gone home," the operator said. "Can I take a message?"

"Just tell him that Mr. Lloyd called—L for Los Angeles, another L, O for—" I was saying when she interrupted, asking, "Mr. Harold Lloyd?"

What greater compliment, I ask you, can New York pay you than to have one of its authorized telephone operators identify your name at first sight?

"Why, Mr. Brunet expects you at nine o'clock to-morrow morning, Mr. Lloyd," she continued. Having no idea that Pathé knew I was in New York, or within less than five days' travel, or cared, this was rolling the old red carpet out for the honored guest and I cannot give Fred Stone all the credit for a merry evening.

"Yes, we have heard all about it," was my greeting from Mr. Brunet at nine A. M., and within half an hour I had signed a new contract calling for an initial salary of $300 a week and containing a provision that Pathé would step in at any time Roach should find the terms of the contract burdensome.

For a week I saw New York at Pathé's expense. They tried to pay the hotel bill and refund my transportation East. I declined, but they already had bought my berth and ticket westward and they insisted on paying the cost of all entertainment. An inaugural dinner was given Mr. Brunet during the week and I found myself at the speakers' table, which is no place to find yourself. And homeward-bound, a Pathé representative traveled with me to complete the contract in Los Angeles.

Roach had put the glasses on Alf Goulding during my absence and made an unsuccessful picture. Alf had played a very funny bit in some emergency in one of the clown pictures. My walkout had left him idle, and Roach, recalling how funny he was as a Swede in a theater gallery, tried him out behind the horn rims. Soon after my return, Goulding walked off the lot without a word and never returned. He was a moody soul and we never have known why he left; if it was thwarted ambition to act again, or wounded vanity, he gave no signs of it.

Stan Laurel and Frank Terry, both of whom had played with Chaplin in Fred Karno's company in England, joined Roach now, and, with Marie Mosquini, made a new comedy unit. Hal directed them while I did the last of the one-reelers by myself —a task made easier by the fact that we still were twelve weeks ahead of schedule even after a month's tie-up, so fast had the Roach-Goulding alternate-week method ground out pictures. Later Terry came over to me as a gag man—the first gag specialist we ever had. He had been one of England's greatest pantomimists and variety comedians, and filed away in his head was every bit of comedy business ever seen in the English music halls, on which he drew endlessly and to our great profit.

By the spring of 1919 the weekly procession of one-reelers had so established the new character with audiences that Pathé suggested that we turn to two-reelers, then regarded as the maximum practicable length for comedies. On April 12, 1919, Roach and Pathé signed a contract for nine two-reel comedies. During the life of this contract, less than a year and a half, the rental charged exhibitors in key cities for first runs rose from $300 on the first, *Bumping Into Broadway,* to $3000 on the final picture—*Number, Please.*

Each was of the same length and approximately the same quality, and there was no remotely corresponding growth in manufacturing costs. The early Lonesome Lukes had cost from $1200 to $1500 to make and the one-reel glass pictures never more than $2000. *Bumping Into Broadway* cost about $30,000; *Number, Please,* less than $40,000. The increased expense on the two-reelers was progressive, but moderate. It was not until we went into three-reel lengths and longer that the cost sheets began to mount dizzily, until now $1,000,000 is not prohibitive.

We wear no more expensive clothes. Raw film costs about the same. Sets are more elaborate, but that is a minor item. Casts are little larger. I still draw only a nominal salary, $1000 a week, taking my return from the profits. Overhead and investment are much greater, but the true inwardness of the enormously increased cost is time; not so much the greater time needed to make five to eight reels as compared with two, but the infinitely greater pains we take with each scene and with the picture as a whole. Originally we shot a scene once and hoped that it was good; now we shoot it from twice to ten times, varying the action and experimenting, and choose the best one for the assembled film.

The jump in first-run rentals from $300 to $3000 in a brief time for two-reel pictures of much the same grade is explained solely by demand. We had sown, plowed and fertilized, and now we reaped. A letter issued from Pathé headquarters to all branch offices on September 24, 1919, just in advance of the release of *Bumping Into Broadway,* throws light on this.

The letter calls attention to the special advertising campaign, including page space in *The Saturday Evening Post,* with which the New Million Dollar Two-Reel Lloyd Comedies are about to be launched and goes on to say:

"Charlie Chaplin, Douglas Fairbanks, Mary Pickford and other big stars whose pictures to-day command big rentals, all had a turning point in their careers—a period in which their pictures jumped from small rentals to prices to which they legitimately are entitled. And the turning point in Harold Lloyd's career now has arrived. You know and we know that in the past the Harold Lloyd comedies were being sold at ridiculously low prices; so low that when on the first of March this year we started raising the prices on one-reel Lloyds, inside of nine days all our branches combined showed an increase on collections for these subjects of 400 per cent without receiving one cancellation."

The letter also called attention to the fact that I had been averaging a comedy a week for five years and was therefore the "most widely circulated comedian of all." It closed with a notice that exhibitors thereafter would be required to book new Lloyd pictures on a separate contract calling for one every twenty-eight days.

With the completion of *Captain Kidd's Kids,* the second two-reel picture, Bebe left us to go to Cecil DeMille. From the time we made the three pictures at San Diego in 1915, she and I had been pretty constant companions, one of our chief bonds of interest a mutual love of dancing. The only formal instruction in dancing I ever had consisted of three lessons in a children's class either in Omaha or Denver, and restricted to step, glide, close; step, glide, close. The balance I picked up on dance floors from girl partners, aided by a good sense of rhythm.

For a year or two before the war, dancing for cups was a craze in the picture colony. Bebe and I won twenty cups or more in competition against Wallie and Dorothy Reid, Gloria Swanson and Wallace Beery and many other movie couples at the Sunset Inn, Santa Monica; the Ship Café, Ocean Park; Nat Goodwin's at Venice, Watt's Tavern and such popular resorts. The management offered the cups, collecting on the heavy patronage attracted both of picture people and the curious, and left the decision to popular vote of the spectators.

We asked no odds of any team, but the award, I am forced to confess, was not always governed strictly by merit. With picture people frequently in the majority, it was not unknown for studio politics to creep in. Sometimes, too, a couple such as Wallie and Dorothy Reid won so often that the fickle audiences rebelled against the monotony of it and bestowed the cup on less nimble feet.

The first car I ever owned was a second-hand flivver bought when we were working on Santa Monica Boulevard and my salary was somewhere between fifty and seventy-five dollars a week. It was one of those cars that had begun life as a flivver, but had been stripped and altered to a semblance of a race car—no fenders, racily rounded hood, round gas tank and trunk on the rear, the whole painted a dark blue. For some reason I had no liking for driving it at first and used to persuade Gil Pratt to take the wheel. Later, Bebe and I made our dancing rounds in it. If it rained, if only the streets were wet, we had to cover ourselves with newspapers, for the fenderless wheels threw up twin cascades of dirty water.

A stock model six-cylinder touring car succeeded the flivver when we were back at Court Street and my salary had risen to $100 a week. When we shifted from Court Street to Norbig, Bebe had moved to Edendale to be near the new studio, and she continued to live there after we moved to the boulevard, then back to Court Street. The route to and from her home took us past the Keystone studio, where Wallie Beery was working and in front of which his car, painted a lovely cerulean blue, usually was to be seen. Black was as standard for automobiles as it was for bridegrooms in that day, and we were so ravished by Wallie's bold plumage that all the joy was gone from the new touring car until I sent it to the shop and shamelessly had the blue paint job copied. At the same time I had the leather replaced with figured mohair upholstery and white wire wheels added. Work stopped at the studio the Saturday morning I first drove the remodeled job up the hill, and the next day, Sunday, Bebe and I paraded every street in Hollywood impartially that no one might be denied a sight of us. Within two or three months there were a dozen or more copies of Beery's blue in town.

Bebe long had had a natural desire to graduate from comedies into dramatic pictures. About a year before she left the company, we were dancing at the Sunset Inn in Santa Monica one night. We survived the elimination contests and defeated the Reids for the cup in the finals. DeMille, his scenario writer, Jeanie Macpherson, and party were there, and the director broached the question of Bebe coming to him. She said she would like nothing better, but that her contract with Roach yet had a year to run.

"I will keep you in mind," he told her, "and when the year is up we will see."

The year passed, and, though we had made two two-reel pictures by then, neither had been released. Practically we still were a one-reel comedy company; the reception of the two-reelers was problematical and Bebe saw no reason to change her belief that dramatic pictures offered her a better future. She had given Roach the usual notice, and when De Mille renewed his offer she left.

As long as she was going, Roach and I agreed that we should seek a sharp contrast in our next leading woman; as Bebe was a brunette, that meant a blonde. Furthermore, we wanted some one fresh and new to pictures. Inquiries at the casting agencies developed no promising leads, but Hal's eye was caught one day by a girl playing the lead in a Bryant Washburn picture. He borrowed a portion of the film, brought it to Court Street and ran it off in our projection room. The girl was young, fresh, pretty and blonde.

"That's the girl; she suits me," I said at once.

Her name was Mildred Davis; but, when we tried to find her through the casting agencies, we struck a cold trail. She had left Hollywood and pictures, several persons told us; but no one knew where she had gone, until finally one agency located her in Tacoma, Washington, where she was attending high school. Mildred was born in Philadelphia of old Quaker stock. Her father, a newspaper circulation promoter, recently had moved his headquarters from Los Angeles to Tacoma. Mr. and Mrs. Davis had argued that Mildred yet was too young to take up pictures professionally and that she should finish her schooling, and she agreed the more readily in that her brief experience in the films had not been particularly exciting. Pictures had been dismissed from her mind for months, when, returning from a trip to Seattle one afternoon, she received Roach's telegram.

If Mildred had ever heard of Rolin she could not remember such a company; and one-reel comedies, which were all that had been released to date, were nothing to get hysterical over; but what girl who had left Hollywood, put pictures out of her mind and taken up her schoolbooks again, could have resisted such honest flattery as this? With her mother and her five-year-old brother she took the first train southward. Her one fear was that Roach would not be prepared for her excessive youth, and in an effort to hide the scantiness of her years she nearly destroyed her opportunity. Before appearing at the studio she bought a new wardrobe—one intended to express maturity. It included a large hat ornamented with a large and wavy plume, and Mildred adjusted her deportment to the grave dignity of the plumage.

Our first meeting was mutually disappointing. She knew little of Harold Lloyd, and, in make-up and character clothes in which we met, I fell something short of her ideal leading man. For my part, I exclaimed to myself, "Can this be the girl in the Washburn picture, or have those roguish little pixies, the telegraph boys, put a changeling in our nest?" The very qualities that had charmed us Mildred had effaced so painstakingly that it was some time before Hal and I realized that it was only her clothes that were wrong.

Mildred made her debut in *From Hand to Mouth,* the third two-reel picture, finished in June, 1919, but not released until 1920; so we had nearly a year to wait before seeing our judgment in her choice confirmed by the public. The following picture, *His Royal Slyness,* was Pollard's last, Snub graduating to the head of a comedy company of his own, under Roach.

Pathé had waited to see the first four two-reelers before deciding on the advertising campaign and the increased rentals mentioned some paragraphs back. Now they called on Roach for a varied selection of still photographs of me, both straight and in comedy poses, for lobby display and promotional purposes. Having no still photographer of our own, an engagement was made for Sunday, August 24, 1919, with a commercial photographer named Witzel at Eighth and Hill Streets.

I was making up in my dressing room in the Bradbury mansion Sunday noon. The property room was in the stable and Frank Terry suggested that he select a few props for use in the comedy poses. The dressing-room window looked out on the stable yard, and Terry, from the stable doorway, would hold up a prop to view, I nodding or shaking my head. He held up a bomb, pantomimed lighting the fuse and using it as a cigarette lighter, and I nodded agreement.

Several of us were members of the Uplifters Club and five weeks before the studio had made two bombs for some stunt suggested by the news from Russia or the war at a club outing at Bear Lake. They were papier-mâché, rounded and painted black to represent the bombs anarchists always are to be seen on the verge of tossing in newspaper cartoons. The property man was not an explosive engineer and overdid the charge. When one shattered a heavy oak table at Bear Lake, the stunt was called off and the other bomb returned to the studio.

All explosives were supposed to be kept under lock at the studio, and how this bomb got into a bin of property grenades, we never have learned. How the fuse came to be changed is more inexplicable. The two bombs made for the Bear Lake outing carried stock fuses. Property grenades are dummies carrying a special fast smoky fuse to heighten the comedy, and the one Terry brought along had such a fuse. He had no thought, of course, of finding a true bomb among the properties, and, had he, his suspicions would have been disarmed by the fuse. The weights of the true and the false varied and I believe that I would have detected the mistake had I gone for the properties myself, but I held the thing in my hand for the first time at the Witzel studio, the fuse already lighted, and my mind on the pose.

The photographer had taken four straight poses, the last a mock tragic farewell expression, when he asked, "Now shall we try some of the gag pictures?"

Terry picked up the bomb, lighted it and handed it to me. I put a cigarette in my mouth, struck a sassy attitude and held the bomb in my right hand, the fuse to the cigarette. The smoke blew across my face so clouding the expression that the photographer, whose head was buried under his black cloth, delayed squeezing the bulb. As he continued to wait and the fuse grew shorter and shorter, I raised the bomb nearer and nearer to my face until, the fuse all but gone, I dropped the hand and was saying that we must insert a new fuse, when the thing exploded.

Had I not lowered my hand at that instant I should have been killed instantly, my head probably blown off. The force of the blast was principally upward. It tore a hole in the sixteen-foot ceiling, burst all the windows and, incidentally, split from end to end the upper plate of a set of false teeth in Terry's mouth. The photographer fainted dead away.

Blinded, bloody and stunned, I staggered outside. A man was just alighting from a small car at the curb.

"Take this man to a hospital quickly!" Terry shouted, steered me into the back seat and followed himself.

The stranger drove furiously to the Methodist Hospital, where they put me to bed in a ward and drew a screen around the cot. The pain by now was excruciating. I have heard that taking ether is a ghastly experience and that patients fight against the anaesthetic. I found it as grateful as a glass of cool water to one perishing of thirst.

The pain was considerable for days, but trivial beside my mental state. In a few weeks my salary was to have been raised to $1000 a week, the boundary between little and big money in films, with one-fourth interest in the pictures—a total of not less than $1500 a week. The first of the two-reel pictures had not yet been released and the possibilities of the glass character were just dawning.

At twenty-six, after six years of incessant hard work and little money, I had stood on the threshold of, to me, breathless possibilities, only to be cut down in a moment by some one's carelessness. I was scarred and torn beyond all thought, of course, ever of acting again before a camera—even on the stage. My eyes were bandaged, but I did not know of the doctors' fears for them and I began to work out a philosophy.

After all, acting was not everything in pictures. As great—yes, greater—successes were open to directors. Direction, come to think of it in a hospital bed, was the great new art of pictures. A real director overshadowed the players; it was he really who wove the pattern of the picture. The name was the same, but a great gulf separated stage direction and film direction. I was only twenty-six, not even married, and had accumulated an invaluable fund of technical experience which could be applied to other things than clowning. Why couldn't I be a director? Darn it! I would be a director and do big things, not necessarily comedies. I had saved some money too.

"What the hell, Bill, what the hell!" my spirits demanded. "Suppose you hadn't lowered your hand?"

Visitors and the hospital staff were startled by the cheerfulness of a man who had just seen a career blow up in his face with heavy damage to both. When I fretted, it was mere impatience, more often than not, at the delay in being up and at it.

In four or five days the doctors found that the left eye was sound. They said nothing to me at the time, for both the consulting eye specialist and the insurance physician were convinced that I would lose the right eye. In another week they told me so. It had been punctured, they said, but it might be possible to preserve its outward appearance.

My face was raw meat and the first efforts were concentrated on preventing gangrene. The antiseptic treatment accomplished its purpose, but, in turn, set up a maddening rash and an outbreak of boils. Then my fearfully swollen lips cracked in four deep crevasses as they began to heal. The boils, the rash and the cracked lips were at least as agonizing as the worst that had gone before, and I cursed the curses of Job.

My own doctor never had despaired of the right eye and time vindicated him. It had not been punctured. The bandages were taken off one day and I was wheeled out on the second-floor veranda of the hospital. I had looked forward eagerly to this day, but suddenly as I saw trees and light and daily life again gloom overwhelmed me. I asked to be taken back in, and lay silent, bitter and rebellious the rest of the day. In the morning the despondency had gone.

Before the accident dad and I had been preparing to move from the Delbert apartments, where we had kept house so long, to a home we had bought at 369 South Hoover Street, a vine-covered, shingled bungalow set in a leafy yard. Dad moved while I was in the hospital, and when they let me leave, it was there I went.

Showers of kindness had fallen daily on my head all the while I was in the hospital from friends and others who knew me only as a shadow on the screen. In a heap of mail one day there was an unsigned card posted at Worcester, Massachusetts. It was just a stock greeting card, reading:

> I've had some awful illnesses,
> And accidents that stretched me flat,
> But anyway I'm still alive,
> And lots of people can't say that.

I don't know about the meter, and the sentiment may lack something of being profound, but I was alive, and finding compensations in that statistically unusual state.

V

The Night Life
of Hollywood

IN AUGUST, 1919, my acting days were done and I was lucky, perhaps unlucky, to be alive. In November, 1919, I walked down Broadway on my second visit to New York and saw "Harold Lloyd" in lights over two theaters. In March, 1920, I was back before the camera, taking up the fifth two-reel picture, *Haunted Spooks,* where the explosion had halted it eight months before.

First my sight was found to be intact. Then the face, that had been a frightful, hopeless thing, healed gradually without a scar. Three or four faint black powder specks are the only mementos left upon it. All in the day's work for the doctors, but quite a chapter in the life of the patient. My gratitude and admiration can be surmised.

While I was convalescing in the new house on Hoover Street, my face still unhealed, John McKeon and the late Hiram Abrams, who subsequently became head of the United Artist pictures, called and offered me a five-year contract at $500,000. I was flattered but incredulous. My lawyers had told me that the accident automatically had voided the contract with Roach and that I was a free agent, if I so wished. As a moral tonic to a man in my fix the offer was magical, but was it anything more than a gesture? Abrams and McKeon were men of standing. On the other hand, contracts always were being waved recklessly in Hollywood and were not always all they seemed.

"Why, I probably never can work again in pictures," I exclaimed. "I don't know whether you are just trying to cheer me up or not; if you are, you have succeeded and I am mighty grateful to you, but how can I talk business in such circumstances?"

"Well, we are willing to gamble half a million on it," McKeon replied. "Evidently we expect to get something for our money.

A Sailor-Made Man (1921) : the laughing gob.

From *Grandma's Boy* (1922), which with *A Sailor-Made Man* raised Harold to Hollywood's first flight.

Grandma's Boy: a prophecy of a marriage to come.

From *Hot Water* (1924).

If you think we are fooling, we can have a lawyer up here in twenty minutes."

I thought that over, hesitated and said: "In the first place, Roach is in New York and I cannot sign anything without first hearing what he has to say. Hal has been fair to me and has first call, I feel. At the same time, yours is a business proposition, and a flattering one, and I'll consider it seriously."

When they had gone I wired Roach the details and told him I should be compelled to accept unless he could advance something comparable. He replied, on his return, with an offer of a partnership on a fifty-fifty basis and to increase my percentage in the four completed two-reel pictures from one-fourth to one-half.

"Each picture ought to net you $25,000 on this basis," he said. "I believe Pathé will be at least as willing as an outsider is to gamble; they have much more at stake, but whether they are or not or whether you ever can work again or not, you still will have $100,000 and a half interest in the business."

It was a generous offer and I accepted it in part. The partnership I declined for the present; if I should be able to work again before the camera I should not wish to be loaded down with business details. A few days later we went to New York together, my second time there, and found Pathé willing, as Roach had predicted, to bet on my recovery. We were only one string on the Pathé bow, but to that extent the accident had been as calamitous to them as to us, and their only hope of salvaging anything lay in carrying on.

The old and interrupted contract was scrapped and a new one written for a term of three years. It called for the completion of *Haunted Spooks* and the four remaining two-reelers of the original program, and for six further two-reel pictures, Pathé to do all financing of production, as in the past. Their return for this and for distribution ranged from 65 per cent of the gross earnings of the Lonesome Luke pictures, gradually revised downward to 37½ per cent on the final contract, made in 1922. The great increase in gross earnings meanwhile much more than made up the difference, of course.

Walking down Broadway alone after dinner of our first evening there, I saw in lights on the marquee of the Strand Theater at Forty-seventh Street, Pauline Frederick in *Bonds of Love*. I stopped with professional interest. Then, with no preparation, I saw in more lights—red, white and blue—over the portal of the theater, "Harold Lloyd in *Bumping Into Broadway*."

You may never have seen the Great White Way and know and care nothing of the theater, and still I need not tell you what it means to any actor to see his name in lights on Broadway for the first time. My heartbeat jingled the coins in my pocket, my legs wavered weakly and I stood staring, mouth open, until I woke to a fear that I might be attracting attention. So, closing my mouth, I strolled back and forth, but never took my eyes from that rainbow. The picture's title had been pure chance. *Bumping Into Broadway!*

"Here! Here! This won't do," returning senses told me. I shook myself together, and, with my heart still playing Sousa's "Stars and Stripes Forever," drove my legs down Broadway. Five blocks below I saw Dorothy Gish's name in lights over the Rialto, then the same "Harold Lloyd in *Bumping Into Broadway*," and I remembered nothing more until the next morning.

The Strand and the Rialto were, in 1918, the two great picture houses of Broadway and this was the first day and date booking of any picture, I believe—certainly of any comedy—in these or any other two leading Broadway theaters. Whether Pathé had played any part in arranging this surprise party, I do not know. They knew of it, naturally, and carefully allowed me to discover it for myself. No, sir, they don't seem to put the same stuff in thrills that they used to.

While I was laid up Mildred and Pollard had carried on at the studio, making one-reel comedies. Back on the job, we resumed *Haunted Spooks* where we had left off and made it, probably, our funniest picture to date. We had been so far ahead of schedule that we never lost a release date, our only difficulty the fact that women's clothes were changing so rapidly just after the war that there was a perceptible gap in skirt lengths in nine months' time.

The last vestige of the old comedy dress vanished from my character with *Haunted Spooks,* and my clothes thereafter were normal street wear, except when the rôle called for costume— that is, whatever I wore from then on was chosen to fit the character, not to draw laughs on its own. In the first four two-reelers I had worn a flowing Windsor tie, cloth-top button shoes, a checked suit, and at times my hats leaned a little toward the comic. I had been wearing the checked suit when the bomb exploded. Little remained of it, but had not a button been missing I still should not have cared to see it again. Thereby the accident speeded up the evolution of the character to a completely straight rôle.

We were the lone remaining studio in downtown Los Angeles now. The city was growing up and traffic was a problem. Increasing municipal restrictions and high rentals had driven all the rest to Hollywood and other suburbs. Further legislation early in 1920 by the city council caused Roach to build a new studio in Culver City. In the midst of *An Eastern Westerner,* the sixth two-reel picture, we moved from Court Street to the new studio.

"I am not superstitious, but—" is the way to begin this paragraph. In private life I do little knocking on wood, but professionally I am an actor, therefore superstitious. My rabbit's feet take the form of a reluctance to change any routine once a picture is under way. I hate to part with a pair of shoes that has served me loyally in a picture. The route that we take from the house to the studio and from the studio to the location lot the first day of a picture is fixed, unless circumstances necessitate a change. Similarly, I found excuses for not leaving the Bradbury mansion until the first sequence of *An Eastern Westerner* was completed.

For days I continued to dress and make up in my old dressing room there and drive the many miles to Culver City, where all the rest had gone. I now owned two cars—one a limousine—and had my first chauffeur valet, a Japanese boy. When the picture was done he and I made a ceremony of quitting the old place where my picture career virtually had begun. We went about bowing and saying farewell to each room, the stable and the yard, a gesture in which Somen joined gravely. To his Oriental mind such deference to inanimate objects was rational and seemly. On the sidewalk we made a final salaam and drove away, and I never have been back.

Roach renewed his offer of a partnership after he had built the Culver City plant, but I preferred to concentrate on my own pictures and, instead, we revised the fifty-fifty division on my pictures. As time went on and Hal devoted more and more of his attention to his other units, this sharing agreement was revised further, finally to 80 and 20 per cent. That is, Pathé first divided the earnings of the pictures with Hal, then he and I split the remainder as stated. So, from having no share in the pictures in the beginning of 1919, I had 80 per cent of the producers' end by the close of 1921. Roach meanwhile continued to advise with me and to work on story material for subsequent pictures.

With *Number, Please,* the ninth two-reeler and the last of the original Pathé contract, Hal ceased to direct me, and Fred Newmeyer, who had been directing girl pictures in another Roach unit, took his place. Newmeyer originally was a southpaw pitcher in the AA leagues. He and his catcher first appeared as extras at the old Universal lot when Roach and I were extras there in J. Farrell Macdonald's unit. Macdonald detailed Billy Musgrove and me to make up Newmeyer, his battery mate and other extras. Later Fred became property boy for Roach, then assistant director, next director of one-reelers. When Hal and I separated, Newmeyer came with me. He still is under contract to the Harold Lloyd Corporation, but now is directing Reginald Denny on loan from us.

The lending of players, directors and cameramen is a commonplace in Hollywood. For example, Jean Hersholt, a high-priced character lead for Universal, was in such demand in 1927 that he worked on loan to other companies all but three or four weeks of the year. The borrower usually pays the lender a bonus—in Hersholt's case as much as double his contract salary of $1750 a week—permitting the lender a handsome profit as well as saving it all salary charges for the period of the loan.

The three high spots in our two-reel career, each marking a brisk advance in story and laughs, were the first, *Bumping Into Broadway, Haunted Spooks* midway, and the seventh, *High and Dizzy,* a thrill picture. The two-reelers were sold first in blocks of six, then in blocks of three to exhibitors, the rental price jumping on each block. Before we moved into the longer lengths most theaters were giving them first billing over the program picture.

Only one of the six additional two-reel pictures specified in the revised Pathé contract stopped at that length. That was the third, *I Do,* which was made in three reels, but cut to two for exhibition. At the first preview in three reels it disappointed so badly that we feared for a moment that it was a total loss. Further inquiry seemed to place the blame on the slowness of the first reel. Experimenting, we threw out the entire first reel, with such satisfactory results that I always have regarded *I Do* as one of our outstanding two-reel films.

The first, second and fourth of the six additional pictures ran three reels, the fifth to four reels and the sixth to five, since when we never have made a picture under five reels. Each was begun with two reels in mind, but, the footage running long and the action and comedy justifying the extra footage, we threw in a reel or more to boot. Pathé was under no contractual obligation to pay us anything additional for this heaping measure. They did so voluntarily. It was not so much, perhaps, as we were entitled to in strict equity—certainly not so much as we could have forced from them by balking—but we preferred to keep faith and to build our future rather than immediate profits.

Thus two of the most successful pictures in our history, *A Sailor-Made Man* in four reels and *Grandma's Boy* in five, both were made under a two-reel contract. I had carried the idea of *Grandma's Boy* in my head for three years and tried to fit it into one- and two-reel lengths, but it would not be squeezed in. Finally I concluded to make it in whatever length it might work out. When it was finished and cut we had five reels, and five good ones, but it had cost us more than $100,000.

Not only were both pictures longer, they were much better in every way. A one-reel film runs only ten minutes; even in two reels there is little room both for establishing character and being funny; and confronted with that choice, it is character that must be sacrificed. Hence one- and two-reel comedies can only be a succession of gags loosely strung on the outline of a story. If the gags are good the picture is good; poor gags, poor picture.

In five reels or more we can be both funny and sincere. When I say sincere, I use it with comedy reservations. Picture comedies cannot be true to life and be funny, for though life can be as funny as all out-of-doors, the comic incidents are separated by long intervals of dull routine, with moments of drama and tragedy. Nature usually is a punk continuity writer. A good picture should crowd more comedy into five to eight reels than happens to most of us in a lifetime.

If it cannot hold a mirror up to life, however, a film comedy can keep within shouting distance of verity. "Is it plausible while you are looking at it?" is the only test it needs pass. It will be only if the characters are plausible. The action may be outlandish, but the characters—most particularly the central character—must not be. Every one in the audience should feel that he knows him, has known him, or might easily know him.

A Sailor-Made Man and *Grandma's Boy* were markers on the most important boundary line in our later history. Two such longer and better pictures, coming together, gave us a mighty thrust forward that carried us out of the middle ground into the foreground of picture business. They demonstrated, too, that the public wanted what we know as feature-length comedies. *Grandma's Boy* was the last of the revised Pathé contract and, when we signed a new one in January, 1922, it called for six pictures of five reels or more. Thus *Doctor Jack,* the first of this contract, was likewise the first premeditated five-reeler.

Safety Last, which followed *Doctor Jack,* was seven reels long. It has its partisans who hold that we never have made a better, and they are not far wrong in my judgment. It was a thrill picture, if you remember my climbing the face of the twelve-story building, and thrill pictures have an unfair advantage over straight comedies.

The old formula for comedy drama of the David Warfield school was "a laugh, a tear and a laugh." The recipe for thrill pictures is a laugh, a scream and a laugh. Combine screams of apprehension with stomach laughs of comedy and it is hard to fail.

Safety Last came of an old family. Its original progenitor was a one-reel glass character picture called *Look Out Below.* For it we built a frame of wooden girders, painted to likeness of steel, two and a half stories high, over the southern portal of the Hill Street tunnel, which the city conveniently had bored through the bluff on which the Bradbury mansion stands. It was our first thrill picture depending upon height for its effects, and was original with us as far as I know. Neither it nor any of its three descendants contained any doubling, double exposure or trick photography in the usual sense. The illusion lay in deceptive camera angles of drop and height.

The second member of the family was a two-reeler called *High*

The opening shot of *Safety Last* (1923), the greatest of the thrill pictures. A typical Lloyd gag: what appears to be the death house is disclosed a moment later as a railway station.

Safety Last: hanging on
to the clock during the
ascent of the building.

Safety Last: the face of
the clock gives way.

Safety Last: suspended above Los Angeles.

Safety Last: danger even on the topmost cornice.

Safety Last: the heroine's presence won't
help matters.

and Dizzy, taken on the same scene, but presumably on the ledge of a completed ten-story hotel instead of bare girders, and having nothing in common with *Look Out Below* except the height theme.

The third generation of the family was *Never Weaken,* a three-reel *de luxe* edition of *Look Out Below.* The thrills came of my efforts to commit suicide in the belief that Mildred had thrown me down. This time we built our framework of girders on the roof of the Ville de Paris department store, the owner of which, Bernal Dyas, is a close friend of Roach. We used the interior of the same store for the department-store scenes in *Safety Last,* the next thrill picture, working from closing time until two and three o'clock the next morning.

The success of the thrill idea in one, two and three lengths suggested trying it at full-program distance. One afternoon in downtown Los Angeles I stopped to watch Bill Strothers, who called himself the Human Spider, scale the sheer walls of a high office building. The higher he climbed the more nervous I grew, until, when he came to a difficult ledge twelve stories up, I had to cut around a corner out of sight of him and peek back to see if he was over the ledge.

If it makes me this jumpy, what would it do to a picture audience, I asked myself. The more I thought of it the better I liked it. Once I feel like this about a story, all the staff like to work on it, for they can count upon my enthusiasm; whereas, if the story is another's and doubts linger in my mind, it takes some of the zest out of my work.

When we have a story to build, the three gag men, the director and I get in the gag room and work it out. All we had to begin with here was the human-fly idea. Obviously I must not be a professional human fly in the picture; if I am an expert there is no comedy in the situation. We would hire Bill Strothers himself for that rôle and I must be a fool boy roped, in some comedy fashion, into climbing the building in Bill's stead, which is a comedy situation. The plot gradually worked out this way: I was to be a country boy new to the city. I get a job clerking in a department store. The pompous floor walker is my enemy. I room with Strothers. He innocently makes an enemy of a policeman. After much comedy business in the store, gags suggested by the locale, I sell the manager on the idea of having a human fly climb the building as an advertising stunt. When the time comes for Strothers to climb, his enemy, the cop, is found to be patrolling the beat in front of the store. He gives chase to Strothers. The store manager impatiently demands to know where my human fly is. The crowd is waiting, and in order to save the situation I reluctantly start the climb for Strothers, who tells me that he will take my place at the second story. But the cop pursues him to the second floor, then to the third and on. Meanwhile I have to continue, finally making the entire ascent myself, the cop having run Strothers to the roof and over an adjacent roof.

Not that we waited to start shooting until we had such a finished plot. All we ask to know when we begin is our general direction. The chinks can be filled in as we go along.

The dizzy drops in the picture were partly illusion. Although you saw the city's traffic crawling many stories below, at no time could I have fallen more than three stories, but who wants to fall three stories for that matter? I have no desire to break my neck and it would be very foolish of me from a business stand-point. All the staff, the company officers, the distributors and others have a like business interest in keeping me alive and whole. So the amount of risk I take in a thrill picture becomes a compromise between the necessity of taking some and the foolishness of taking too much.

As it was, I threw my shoulder out of joint in the scene—probably the loudest scream of the picture—where I grab frantically at the minute hand of the building clock, many stories up, and the face of the clock is pulled out and down by my weight. At Ocean Park, one night just after we had finished this sequence of *Safety Last,* a party of us stopped at a fortune teller's booth. The reader of the stars felt the calluses of my hands and told me that I earned my living at manual labor. She was not far wrong.

We must guard against sameness in my character. I should not be the same type of boy in two successive pictures. The original idea of *Why Worry,* suggested by the Coué every-day-in-every-way epidemic then raging, called for me to be a wealthy young hypochondriac, in contrast to the poor but healthy country boy of *Safety Last* seeking his fortune in the city.

A rich boy is off to a poor start with any audience and if, in addition, he goes about with a clinical thermometer under his tongue and counting his own pulse, who cares what happens to him? The idea is all right, however, for the first several reels. In these you establish the character and have fun with him. A child should be able to fill in the balance of the picture. Manifestly you must drop your young man rudely into a situation where his money counts for nothing, slam the health into him and the nonsense out of him. This done, and the audience will adopt him even if he still has his money left in the final fade-out, but, if you believe in Safety First, strip him of his chattels and let the heroine be riches enough for any man.

Seeking a situation where my money would not count, the plot carried me off to a fictitious Central American country; then, having me there and in difficulties, the plot suddenly demanded a giant. So the late George Auger of the Ringling circus was engaged to giant for us. His circus engagements would keep him busy for two months more and we went ahead with the early reels. Two were completed and Auger was leaving New York for Los Angeles the next day, when he fell dead in his hotel.

Inasmuch as we had not yet used him before the camera, there was no footage to be thrown away, and plenty of big men were to be had by calling up the casting bureau. Auger, however, had not been a big man but a giant, and the plot called for a giant, no less. We advertised widely, instructing applicants to send photographs, which they did in numbers, but the photographs proved nothing. Any man of more than six feet looks impressive alongside another of four feet and most of our applicants had sought out the smallest man in the community as a foil. In the midst of the search some one on the staff saw a newspaper story about an extraordinary pair of shoes made by some cobbler for a giant in Minnesota. Looking up the name in our files, we found that the man had answered our advertisement, sending a photograph. The picture was worthless, for it had been taken against a background that contained nothing by which to measure his height.

Roach was going to New York and he made an appointment to meet the Minnesotan in Chicago. The man proved to be as tall as Auger had been, and much heavier framed, and Roach dispatched him to us forthwith. Auger had owned a voice that goes with a giant. When the new man opened his mouth, the anticlimax was terrific, his voice was so soft and high-pitched.

Mildred had been with us for three years and her contract would expire when *Safety Last* was finished. Offers of more money and dramatic rôles were coming to her from other producers. We could meet the money terms, possibly, but we could not offer her the wider opportunities of general picture work, and so could not quarrel with her decision to leave.

It needed the prospect of losing her to bring home to me the fact, apparent for months to every one else from the increasing ardor of my devotion, that I loved her. Mildred paid me the handsome compliment of giving up a future in dramatic pictures by saying yes, and we were married in the midst of *Why Worry*.

The press agents rather than the clergy, it seemed to us, had been solemnizing too many of the marriages in Hollywood. That was not the marriage we wished. Aside from Mildred's mother, her bridesmaid and my brother and best man, Gaylord, we told no one. My infatuated conduct, I fear, told others and, for all my threats, the possibilities for newspaper space presented by a wedding were too rich for the blood of Joe Reddy, our publicity director. His sacerdotal dignity deceived me for long, but I learned eventually that he had notified the newspapers. Reporters were on guard in front of her home when Mildred prepared to leave for the church. She hid on the floor of the car and told the chauffeur to drive her to my home, and escaped them, but when we came in sight of the church half a dozen reporters and cameramen were sitting on the steps. Turning down a side street, we drove away, to return later in the afternoon. They were still waiting. On our promise to pose as much as they liked after the ceremony, they left us alone at the altar. Earlier in the day there had been a fashionable wedding in the church and it still was banked with gorgeous flowers, to which we fell heir.

That evening we drove to San Diego and let the picture wait. San Diego left us beautifully alone. Once in the dining room of the U. S. Grant Hotel we feared exposure. Bill Russell saw us, his eyes lighted up and he bore down upon us. We leaped to our feet and began dancing, but it turned out that Bill merely was glad to see us and knew nothing of our wedded state. After ten days we came back to Los Angeles and an Ambassador Hotel

Why Worry (1923): the giant who filled the number 15 shoes of the late George Auger.

Why Worry:
the hypochondriac and
the giant.

Why Worry: trouble in Latin America.

Why Worry: the insouciant idler.

bungalow, where we were not discovered for several days more.

Two weeks was all the honeymoon the picture would permit and I returned to work. We lived a week in the old home on Hoover Street before making the discovery, common to all young couples, that three or more are a crowd. We planned to rent and the studio looked up half a dozen possibilities. One was a house on Irving Boulevard, Los Angeles, that we liked so well we bought it. We still live there, though we are building a new home in Beverly Hills.

When *Safety Last* was finished Jobyna Ralston, who had been working in Roach one-reel comedies, came in as leading woman in Mildred's stead.

Why Worry was the last picture to be made under the Roach banner. By contract I had the exclusive use of the big stage at Culver City and first call on everything, including Hal's time. He was trying to work four or five other units on the one remaining stage and we came to a point where his own best interests, he agreed, dictated turning me loose.

It was the friendliest possible severance after nearly ten years of teamwork. Roach is, of course, an active independent producer at Culver City to-day. He continues to own an interest in all the glass character pictures up to *Girl Shy,* including the one-reelers, in which last I have no share. Reissued in recent years by Pathé, they have grossed five times their original earnings. All Lonesome Luke pictures were sold outright to Pathé, but they are small loss to us. Of the films made before Luke, I never have seen or heard of any excepting *Just Nuts,* which won the contract with Pathé.

As we were finishing *Grandma's Boy* I had brought into the organization William R. Fraser, who for years had been supervisor of the Federal Forestry Service in the Rocky Mountain district, to handle all my personal business. He is my mother's brother. I had tried to manage my own finances and Fraser, a trained business man, took off my shoulders a burden for which I had neither taste nor training, and which was demanding more and more time that I preferred to give to the picture and to plain enjoying myself.

When the agreement with Roach ended, Fraser directed the organization of the Harold Lloyd Corporation, with himself as secretary and general manager, my father as vice-president and treasurer, and I as president. Since then he has relieved me entirely of a responsibility which I feel no actor can carry success-fully. John L. Murphy, who had been associated with me for years in the Roach organization, joined us as production manager.

It is not necessary to build a studio in Hollywood in order to make pictures. There are various fully equipped and staffed picture plants which can be rented in whole or in part, with technical services if desired. We rented ground space in one of these, the Metropolitan, but built our own sets and offices, brought in our own technical equipment and technicians, and are completely independent of the studio proper.

We finance ourselves without resort, even, to bank loans. Such independence demands a large cash account, but indepen-dence always is worth more than it costs. We have nearly $750,000 tied up in *Speedy,* our current picture as I write this, and it is not finished. Had we had to borrow we might have been under pressure before now to complete the picture, good or bad. Good pictures have been made to specifications, time and cost sheets, like an engineering job, but they are far be-tween and few.

Insufficient capital and credit wreck picture companies, de-partment stores and cigar stands impartially. Two independent producers start shooting stories on $100,000 cost estimates each. Midway, each picture demands another $100,000. The first pro-ducer, his credit exhausted, completes the film within the esti-mate or his creditors take over his business. If the former, the picture returns a minor profit, perhaps a loss. It fails to make a valuable new star or injures the drawing power of an old one, and it damages the business or professional reputations of all concerned. The second producer can command the capital to give his story the production it requires. The picture's earnings are many times the additional $100,000 spent, it makes a new star or enhances an old one, and reflects credit on producer, director and all. But no business man needs a diagram of so everyday a problem.

Decidedly, something more than money is needed to make good pictures; ability must be assumed. However much time and money we may spend, we no longer can hope to pyramid each picture in laughs and interest as we could once. If we do make them better it will be headwork. Capital, however, protects us from any necessity of releasing a bad picture. Should we make a bloomer one of these days, no one but us will see it. However bad, it could be sold readily enough, for many exhibitors buy any standard film merchandise sight unseen. It will be burned, nevertheless, and charged off to profit and loss that the exhibitors may continue to take our quality for granted.

Girl Shy, in eight reels, was the Harold Lloyd Corporation's first picture. When *Grandma's Boy*, four pictures earlier, cost more than $100,000, we were a little startled. *Girl Shy* cost four times that, but on the other side of the ledger it grossed nearly $2,000,000, fifteen to eighteen times the earnings of the early two-reelers.

Grandma's Boy had told much more of a story then we ever had put in a picture before. It was a psychological study of a boy, cowardly both physically and morally, transformed by a fable invented on the spur of the moment by his despairing grandmother, and a magic charm that was, in reality, only an old umbrella handle. Before the end the boy discovers, of course, that he triumphed only because he believed in himself. The story permitted the working of some Civil War costume sequences, a novelty in comedies. So much psychology was rather a daring experiment at the time, but the picture was an enormous success and in *Girl Shy* we told a story, different in plot, but similar in method, again with great success.

Naturally both had to be funny in the bargain, but we placed less dependence upon gags than in the usual picture. These two contrasted types of comedies have come to be known on the lot as "story pictures" and "gag pictures," respectively. The newspaper and magazine reviewers, usually kind to us, are partial to the former. That and the uniform success to date of story pictures has had its influence on my staff. "Let's make this another story picture," I hear on all sides when a new job is taken up. "I don't know about that; let's make them laugh this time," I am inclined to argue.

I like the story pictures as well as any one, yet I am a little afraid of overdoing them and forgetting one of these days that we are makers of comedies. Critical approval is pleasant but heady stuff. A teaspoonful after meals, say, will aid the digestion. In larger doses it has been known to set up delusions of grandeur.

Girl Shy was six months in the making and, except for *Hot Water,* the next one, we have not made a picture in less time since. *Hot Water* ran only five reels, and, coming as it did between two longer, better films, it is little remembered. *The Freshman* followed it, grossing nearly $3,000,000—a figure we have not yet exceeded, though we will approximate it. A number of precincts still are missing on *The Kid Brother* count, but it will approach the *Freshman* mark.

The Freshman was a long overdue ship. As far back as 1915, when I first began to grope about for something better than Lonesome Luke, I had a dim outline in my mind of a college-boy character, but discarded it as too limited in scope. A college picture, even a college series, would be well worth trying, I was convinced, but I did not care to go on being a freshman for life, and that would be the risk. When the glass character finally evolved, I thought of him as of an age and type that could be fitted easily into a college story and intended to make one in one reel, then in two reels. One thing and another sidetracked it; meanwhile the number of students in colleges and the public interest in college football grew tremendously, and when we did make it at last in seven reels we made it most opportunely.

Have you heard, perhaps, of the Night Life of Hollywood? I thought as much. Then you may as well know the rest of it. You public are a fickle, capricious lot and it is guessing what you want that keeps Hollywood up at nights when it should be catching some sleep before the alarm goes off at seven A. M. Such an unknown quantity are you that, when you show that you like a picture particularly, all Hollywood hurries to make more of the same kind before your eyes start roving again.

Jim Cruze makes *The Covered Wagon* for Paramount and every other producer pounds the table and demands to know why his hired help can't make something like this instead of the same old rice pudding, and more to that effect. Whereupon a wave of glorified Westerns follows in the wake of the *Wagon.* The conjunction of Valentino and *The Sheik* disturbs the peace of mind of countless husbands and a week later every juvenile in Hollywood has his order in for a burnoose and a milk-white Arabian charger. The war was supposed to be taboo. M-G-M, taking a tip from the stage and fiction, prove that it is far from so with *The Big Parade,* and several producers are killed in the

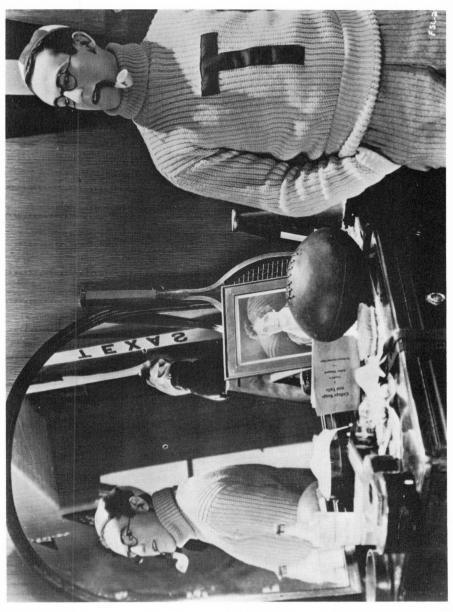

The Freshman (1925):
the college boy's room.

The Freshman: being measured for the prom suit.

The Freshman: having the suit basted.

The Freshman: at the prom the suit disintegrates.

The Freshman: Harold mistakes the severed leg of the tackling dummy for his own.

The Freshman: a lesson
from the coach.

The Freshman: retrieving the ball.

The Freshman: eager to get into the game.

The Freshman:
the great game.

The Freshman:
hero of the hour.

rush. A German director and a German star make a striking picture and six months later the gutters of Hollywood are running with gutturals. One successful costume picture soon has every one but Rin Tin Tin in hose and doublets. So with *The Freshman.* It set off a whole procession of college-football pictures.

Imitation, I realize, is lowly esteemed and no one would care to have it carved on his tombstone, but it pays dividends often where originality tacks a legal notice on the door. Not, of course, that a picture following in the vogue of another necessarily is an imitation. *What Price Glory?* for example, stands very well on its own legs.

The Freshman completed the third contract with Pathé and was the last picture of mine they distributed. Pathé had been my distributor uninterruptedly from the first Lonesome Luke. Since April, 1919, we had made twenty-one pictures of two reels or more for them, to mutual satisfaction. During the life of the third contract, the American Pathé business was sold to Merrill, Lynch & Company, New York stock brokers.

When the time came, in October, 1924, to renew, we asked for a picture-to-picture contract, an increased percentage, a special sales force and lesser concessions, our warrant being the constant and greatly increasing revenue of the pictures. The first really was not a concession, as we saw it, but a mutual advantage. We would be gambling on making a good picture, they on selling it to best advantage. If we made a poor one, they could cancel; if we found their distribution slack, we could cancel.

Merrill-Lynch objected to some of these conditions and sent officers of the company to Hollywood to discuss a compromise. The conference was amiable but arrived nowhere, and finally we played a round of handball and called it off. Paramount offering us everything we asked, we signed a picture-to-picture contract with them and now have made our third film under their banner.

It is nearly universal practice to shoot all scenes with two cameras grinding simultaneously and side by side. In stunt pictures or any scene dangerous or costly to reënact, as many as ten cameras may be used, partly as a precaution, partly to catch the action from varying angles. The second camera in routine picture work was, I suppose, a precaution against the exhaustion of the film magazine of the first camera in the midst of a scene and like emergencies. Inasmuch as it produced a second complete negative, it came to be customary to set this aside for foreign sales and call it the export negative—that is, all films exhibited in North America are struck from the master negative, kept in our vaults. Films sold abroad either are made here from the export negative and shipped to foreign markets or the second negative itself is sent to a European office and copied there, depending somewhat on customs tariffs.

We have used two cameras ever since the first glass-character two-reelers. The variation between the two negatives is very slight. Nowadays, when we retake every scene several times, each completed negative is a selection of the best shots, separately cut and edited, but twins that only the cutter can tell apart. In the earlier days, when we worked on a hurried reel-a-week schedule, we rarely stopped to reënact a scene unless one of the cameras failed during the action.

Our foreign sales were so unimportant that we gave them no thought. What small change did come in from that source was so much velvet, yet not enough velvet to impress us. When the second camera failed occasionally and we were forced to redo a scene, the command was: "Come on now; let's make a quick one for the Eskimos."

Since then, like the rest of American industry, we have discovered the export trade. Foreign sales grew steadily after the war until, with *For Heaven's Sake,* the first Paramount picture, their revenue began to approach the domestic earnings and we look for the foreign market to equal and pass the home market one of these years.

Not only do we no longer slight the second camera but we mind our Perus and Quebecs. If any character is to be held up to scorn or ridicule, let him be unmistakably a citizen of the U. S. A., preferably of old native stock, or else a resident of Mars, where we do not yet sell pictures. The National Association of Police Chiefs makes no protest about the Keystone cops, but the army of Graustark brooks no horseplay with its uniform. Knowing that the pictures are our very own, we rarely read a racial, national or professional slur into the accidents of narrative and characterization. Very broadminded of us, but suppose, just for the sake of supposing, that London made the world's pictures.

Suppose again that a British company should make a good British version of Hoyt's good old American farce, *A Milk White Flag*, which made fun of our politics and our militia. There would be rioting in the armories and hot words in the legislatures, or I don't know my human nature. I can take a joke on myself, perhaps, but I prefer to do the telling of it.

The double L Welsh name of Lloyd bites the foreign tongue that tries to say it and local substitutes once were common. This, however, fails to explain why, up to a few years ago, I was known in Great Britain as Winkle. It appears to have had something to do with the glasses, but just what never has been successfully explained to me. Lonesome Luke was translated as Lui in France, as Lucas and Cinema Lucas in Latin America, and both names carried over to some extent to the glass-character pictures. Although my own name now, apparently, has replaced all others, in Germany and Austria I used to be billed with magnificent simplicity as Er, meaning He, third person, singular number, masculine gender. There is even less in a name than Juliet argued, however. The glasses are the common denominator.

When the fan mail was not so heavy as now dad used to save an occasional letter for the scrapbooks. Most of them are from Japan and the Philippines, which is easily explained. Letters from other non-English speaking countries usually have to be translated. In Japan and the Islands, English has come to be the secondary language and literate Japanese and Filipinos scorn to address an American in any tongue but his own. Their mastery of grammar and vocabulary is admirable, but book taught; their idiom frequently is all their own. As one who speaks no language but mine own, and that indifferently well, my grins are in poor taste when I read a letter from Mr. Dominador Velez, clerk of Cebé, P. I. He writes:

> Will you please send me a picture of Mr. Harold Lloyd, the man who tickles me sometimes breathlessly at the cine show? I had never remembered a comedy act of Mr. Lloyd at the screen which kept me still in my seat, but instead it shook me helplessly with my mouth wide open in laughing. When his name appears in the program I always go to the show one hour ahead of time, for I know the Cebu community will surely break the accommodation or building.

Mr. N. Masuda of Ozaka writes on February 22, 1920:

> *My dear Optimismic Mr. Harold Lloyd:* Allow me to send
> my sincere greeting on the Wothington Birthday to my dear
> modern Wothington of the Comedy Land and to congratulate
> with your constant success after pleasant recovery of your
> wound.
>
> It is, indeed, so long time since I found you in Keystone
> after Universal and Edison, that I have enjoyed appreciating
> many of your Rolin Productions from *Take a Chance* with a
> big promise. Your charaterizing humor manliness is unique
> which never can find in any other Comedians and, moreover,
> your versatile creative talent is absolute compare with that of
> Mr. Chaplin, I think. I am fond of that as well as your splendid
> personality.
>
> In Japan I am now managing editor of the Cinema Taste
> and if you favor me your autographed photograph in token of
> rememberance, though it is too impudent to beg you. I am
> very much happy and pleased to able to adorn our magazine
> thanks to your favor.

I am afraid Mr. Masuda is pulling my honorable leg. Neither
he nor any one else remembers me in Keystone and Universal,
let alone Edison, but with true Oriental courtesy he feels that
he should have remembered me and declines to permit rude facts
to intrude on amenity.

Sgr. José Augusto de Fasedo Fudella of Lisbon, exception to
the rule that Portuguese fan letters usually have to be translated,
writes:

> *My Dear Actor:* Being a constant cinema goer, I have admired
> always your artistic style of playing, so that soon I see in the
> cinema bills notice that is presented a film rehearsed by you,
> I am there. I should like to own a picture of my dear Preferred
> Actor if possible autographed. Can you grant this sincere desire
> from your fervent admirer?

My preference, however, is for a letter that came five years ago
from the dean of the Idaho School of Mines at Moscow, Idaho,
who wrote that his young son, Richard Thomson, had been to
see *Grandma's Boy*. That night Richard closed his evening
prayer with "Please, God, bless grandma and Harold Lloyd, for
Jesus' sake, Amen."

VI

Recipe for a Laugh

How do you make a picture comedy? You don't; it grows like Topsy. Consider the checkered history of *Speedy,* the current picture. The title is a nickname of my own. My father saw a vaudeville act years ago which contained a boy named Harold. His uncle persisted in addressing him as Harold, the boy whining each time, "Don't call me Harold; call me Speedy." Dad pinned the name on me and we became Foxy and Speedy. When the character of the current picture began to take shape, it was seen that the name fitted him like a glove. Moreover, Speedy is brief and suggestive; therefore an intrinsically good title.

There is almost no vestige left in *Speedy* of the original idea— an underworld story. Its origins date back before *For Heaven's Sake;* we wanted a big-city picture as a change, and began with a plot of New York politics, gangsters and such. It called for a girl who should live with a grandfather or an uncle. What occupation for the uncle? Cobbler? Harness maker? Delicatessen dealer? We were searching, you see, for a shop rich in gag possibilities. Some one suggested that the grandfather drive a horse car. A horse car is quaint, has been little used in pictures, and provokes comedy of itself. There had been a horse-car line in New York until recently, operated to hold a franchise. This suggested a plot to steal the franchise from the old man, permitting me to step in, thwart the conspiracy and win the girl, after the usual misadventures. The franchise plot grew until it crowded out the original underworld story.

But it called for a set that would cost $80,000 and for a trip to New York. The season was unfavorable for working in New York, so we filed the story away and adapted the underworld faction into *For Heaven's Sake.* Faction, by the way, is our term for a sequence within a picture—any set of incidents turning on a common theme or locale. Gag, of course, is a comedy bit; for a specific description, follow on.

After *For Heaven's Sake* we took up *The Kid Brother,* an idea we had been holding since the Roach lot. That done, we considered four different stories. One was a ship plot, another a shoe-store idea. We discarded both and a third, then took up a story of a reporter who, through a confusion of names, is thought to have inherited a fortune. The basic comedy lay in the suddenly changed attitude of his fellow townsmen, the deference paid him and the credit extended him until, when the error is discovered, he is ruinously in debt. There were no end of complications and the story declined to jell. After several wasted weeks, I said, "Get out the old file, boys, and let's see what we have left."

The "boys" are Johnny Grey, Howard Emmet Rogers, Lex Neal, Ted Wilde and Jay A. Howe, the story and gag men. I sit with them as frequently as possible. They may have agreed upon a story or have five more or less hostile plots, and I may like all or none, or parts of this and that. The result usually is a compromise so scrambled that no one and every one can claim the authorship.

Our lack of method is deplorable, but somehow it works. Take a hypothetical case. We need a new story. "How about a railroad picture?" one suggests. We canvas the idea, agree and set to thinking in terms of railroading. Let's have the boy a country station agent, baggage man and telegrapher, but the telegrapher suggests a lineman and the lineman suggests a telephone story. A bank robbery is written into the telephone story as an incident. It grows until railroad, telegraphy and telephone all are crowded out and the boy who started to be a country station agent winds up as a bank clerk.

These sessions have been known to be heated and passers-by to duck in passing the gag-room window. Plots are the children of their authors, and parents are prone to resent any insinuation that their offspring are not 100 per cent healthy, handsome and brilliant. "What do you mean, that no board of directors would authorize such a blank check?" demands such a parent in defense of an aspersed detail. "It is done every day. If you want to pick sand out of sugar, how about that comic street-light idea of yours? They haven't used carbon arc lamps for street lighting

from *For Heaven's Sake* (1926).

Speedy (1927): the flip city youth.

Speedy: a **Hollywood** replica of Sheridan Square, New York.

The Kid Brother (1927): authorizing the medicine show.

The Kid Brother: saving Mary from the masher. The girl is played by Jobyna Ralston.

From *Feet First* (1930),
an early Lloyd talkie.

for fifteen years. And while we are on the subject of relentless realism, a model T Ford fires on a magneto, not a battery, as you innocently suppose. What becomes of your battery gag now?" With further comment, both technical and personal, but all hypothetical, naturally.

What type of boy I am to play is the next problem after the broad outline of the horse-car plot is drafted. *Speedy* being a big city picture, I am an irresponsible, flip, scatter-brained, base-ball-crazy youth of a kind the city breeds by the thousands. Now we have the character of the boy, the substance of the dramatic plot and the boy and girl for the love theme. All that remains is to add the comedy and stir vigorously, but that all is every-thing. Plot, love story, novelty are so many sprigs of parsley to dress the dish; the proof of the pudding is in the laughing, and we want "comedy factions with a lot of hooks on them," as we express it.

The character of the boy suggests one group, the plot another group. He is baseball crazy; that gives us a baseball faction in the course of which we employ Babe Ruth and shoot scenes at the Yankee Stadium. Speedy is a lad of many jobs. We have him drive a taxi and work in a drug store for two more factions. For another, we send him to Coney Island with his girl. They go and come on the Subway, and the Subway is a comedy all by itself, except to those who have to ride in it. Likewise the horse car. The horse-car barn is used by the tradesmen of the neighborhood as a clubhouse. The franchise conspiracy threat-ens their clubroom and they rise heroically to the defense of their pinochle game, for another comedy faction.

Soon we have more gags—and good ones—than we possibly can crowd into the picture. Some we discard without trial, others will be edited out. Some were worked out in the gag room, others were born of spontaneous combustion in the midst of camera operations. We finish the greater part of the comedy factions before we turn back to the neglected plot. For example, we began work on *Speedy* in midsummer. At Christmas, the picture three-fourths or more finished, we first turned our minds to devising an opening sequence, and not until a month later did we consider how to end the story.

All of the baseball and Subway, virtually all of the taxi and Coney Island, and much of the horse-car faction were made in

New York and the picture completed in the studio and on location on the Coast. On undeveloped acreage we own in Westwood Hills we built a replica of the Sheridan Square neighborhood on the lower West Side of Manhattan. Some of the picture was taken in the true Sheridan Square, some of it in this California reproduction, and it will need a 20-20 eye to tell them apart in the film. Such salvage as this costly set produces will be in the form of rentals for occasional use by other companies.

The taxi faction is a good example; let's take it apart and see how it works. Three or four ways of opening it occurred to us. We chose one which would let the audience in on the joke. Speedy, out of work again, reads a want ad calling for a "Taxi driver; must be steady and reliable." That, as the audience already knows, is precisely what Speedy is not, and it snickers in anticipation. Speedy next is seen at the wheel of his cab in the garage doorway, listening to the parting instructions of his boss. There is an oil cart in front of the garage, an Out of Order sign hung on it. As Speedy drives away, the right-hand door handle of his cab hooks the sign and carries it off. That is a gag. It is a good gag because it lays a train of comedy and because it could happen to any taxi driver. We took the scene half a dozen times and I did not fail once to hook the sign. Another employee could have hung it on the cab in mischief or jealousy, but that is neither as simple nor as essentially funny as its accidental transfer.

A fade-out designates a lapse of time, and the picture fades in to show the taxi at the curb, Speedy yawning and hunched in his seat and passers-by glancing at the cab, then going on. The audience, knowing what is wrong, enjoys itself at his expense. It is an accepted rule of comedy that the laugh of laughs is one that sneaks up behind the audience and catches it off its guard. There are exceptions, and, no matter how long you have made comedies and studied audiences, you canot be sure always whether it is better to surprise the spectator or to take him into your confidence. In this case, had we not shown the transfer of the sign the audience would be as puzzled as is Speedy at his lack of business; its attention would stray and the eventual surprise would suffer.

A gag in *The Kid Brother* instances a surprise laugh. The heavy slams me against a bulkhead, holds me there and beats me over the head with a belaying pin until it bends with the force of the impact. As he lets go, bewildered at the hardness of my head, I turn and disclose, just above my head, an iron bracket which had caught the blows. The surprise is feasible here for two reasons: The action is fast and the blows are funny in themselves. Thus the audience is alert and already laughing when overtaken by the unexpected dénouement. We made the scene both ways, but preview audiences laughed so satisfactorily at the surprise that we never showed the other version.

There is one rule of comedy that has no exception—you must never disappoint an audience by leading it to expect something that is not in the picture, unless you give it a still funnier situation instead. The original version of *The Freshman* contained a perfect instance of this. In an emergency the boy goes to the Junior Prom in a basted suit of evening clothes. As he dances, the suit begins to unravel. The easiest laugh in the world is to rob a man of his pants in public—so easy that we were above doing it here. The unraveling stopped with his coat.

Frances Marion and other wise old heads who saw the film in our projection room warned me: "Harold, you've got to lose your pants." We continued superior to such hokum, however.

Each picture is previewed three or four times in as many theaters in the Los Angeles district. The theaters are chosen carefully to provide audiences of markedly contrasted types, and the picture is not edited finally until we have tested the responses of these varied cross sections of the picture public. At each preview of *The Freshman* the audience demonstrated that it was looking forward eagerly to the pants following the coat, and, when they did not, made its disappointment so manifest that, after the lapse of a month, we had to redress the set, call back the cast, including many extras in the ballroom scene, and unravel the trousers.

Reverting to Speedy. He calls "Taxi!" at length to a man who glances at the cab, then starts on. The man points to the sign. Speedy leaps to the walk, snatches off the sign indignantly and assures the passenger that it is a mistake. But as he throws in his clutch the car bucks, then dies. He has forgotten to release his hand brake. The passenger alights in disgust and replaces the sign on the door. Another gag.

The taxi faction was designed to run about 600 feet, but grew, in the making, to 1500 feet, or nearly two reels of successive failures to attract a paying passenger. Speedy sets to cruising for fares. A man emerges from an apartment house, a suitcase in each hand, and signals for a cab. Speedy pulls up. A second man dashes out of the apartment house. He is the landlord and the departing guest has not paid his bill. As I load the bags into the cab the landlord knocks the absconder down. I take one look and return the bags to the sidewalk. The guest arises and knocks the landlord down. I replace the bags in the cab. But the guest is knocked down a second time and stays there. The bags return to the walk and stay there.

Two new passengers run up and demand to be taken to the Pennsylvania Station in a hurry. That is the way I take them, pursued, unknown to me, by a motorcycle cop. I pull up at the Penn Station with squealing brakes. The two men burst out of the cab and are off on the run. When I yell, "Hey! Where's my fare?" they turn for an instant, flash detective badges, and vanish into the station. As I sit mourning a fare I must pay out of my own pocket, the outraged motorcycle cop pulls up and gives me a ticket and a dressing down. For my story about the detectives he awards me the razzberry.

He leaves and an old gentleman—a paying fare at last—makes for my cab, but at that moment the detectives reappear, brush the old man aside and give me an uptown address. I wave the ticket at them. "Look at this mess you got me in." They tell me to forget the ticket; they will square that. Meanwhile step on it in the name of the city of New York. This is opportunity! I charge up Eighth Avenue stiff-arming trucks, shaving street cars, scattering pedestrians, ignoring semaphores and lights and pursued again by the motorcycle cop. I look back and shake my teeth at him derisively.

But as the audience knows, and I do not, at the moment I was pushing down the flag, the two detectives had sighted the crook they had been chasing. They leaped from the cab and the old gentleman took their place. When the motorcycle cop finally runs me down, I merely jerk my thumb back to where the two detectives should be riding and ask him to tell his troubles to his superiors. Instead of which, the old gentleman, a nervous wreck from his wild ride, stumbles out of the cab and denounces me as an assassin.

However many the extras or elaborate the pains you take, it is impossible to manufacture a crowd or a traffic scene as convincing as the real thing. The best effects usually are had by mixing the genuine and the synthetic. In *The Freshman* we took some of the footage at the actual California-Stanford game in the Berkeley Stadium, with a full sweep of the great crowd; then duplicated the background as nearly as was feasible by taking the rest of the football faction in a Los Angeles stadium and filling a section of the seats with extras.

The difficulty about tying actual crowd and street scenes up with a picture is that the public should not be aware of the camera. If they are, they stop, stare and grow self-conscious. The enlisting of a crowd without its knowledge is called "stealing a shot." We stole several shots at Coney Island for *Speedy* with much success and attempted to steal another in Times Square.

The police department gave its sanction, an actor in regulation police uniform took up station at Forty-third Street and Seventh Avenue and the two cameras were concealed in a laundry wagon which was to be parked at the curb. When we were ready, another car was found parked in the selected spot. We appealed to the actual traffic policeman on the corner. He ordered the car away, but its four occupants drew back their coats, disclosing police badges. They were city detectives on watch for a thief who, they knew, would stroll up Broadway sooner or later that day. The scene was postponed; then, as we were about to begin a second time, a bundle-laden woman shopper approached our movie policeman for information and refused to be shooed away. The efforts to get rid of her tipped off the crowd and made any further attempt impossible that day, so the bit was put aside to be taken in Los Angeles.

I had remained in a closed door car until the director called, but when I mingled with the crowd I was not recognized until its attention had been caught by the woman-shopper episode. Ted Wilde, the director, was struck by this. I bet him that I could walk down any two blocks of Fifth Avenue in daylight and in make-up, and go unrecognized, and won the bet, though he chose the most difficult stretch of the Avenue—Forty-first to Forty-third streets. I fixed the time at 4 P. M. and Wilde and others followed in a car. Two tricks account for my escape. The first is to lower the eyes. Once you catch the eye of any one, he may start in sudden recognition. The other trick is the time of day. At four o'clock there are no promenaders or idlers on the Avenue. As the business day nears its close every one is bound somewhere in a hurry and preoccupied with his business.

In Los Angeles, in December, we set up a dummy Subway kiosk on a corner in a neighborhood business center, assembled a crowd of extras and a fleet of automobiles with fake New York license plates and made the postponed bit which called only for Speedy to stop, tie a shoe string on the running board of a parked car, go on, and, finding the traffic signal against him, reach out, seize the traffic cop's whistle, blow a blast and proceed through the parting waves. But no amount of dressing will make a suburban intersection in California look like Times Square.

Because taxi rates are about twice as high in California as in New York, the cabs in the fleet were our own and carried the characteristic "15 and 5" of New York. It is cheaper to maintain a few old taxis than to repaint rented cabs. Passenger cars may be hired at the usual livery rates, of course, but the cost of any equipment not regularly let out for hire is a considerable expense in movie production. Ten per cent a week of the retail price is the customary rental fee. For example, a bit in a dentist's office demands a full, modern dental outfit. We use it three or four days and pay one-tenth of what it would cost a dentist outright. If it is scratched or damaged in any way we pay additionally. There are large furniture houses in Hollywood which do not sell $100 worth of goods a week; their business is almost exclusively the renting of furnishings to the studios, while the Los Angeles Costume Company has become the world's greatest costume house.

After shooting this whistle trifle we spent the balance of the day touring residential Los Angeles, extras and all, seeking a location for the even smaller shoestring bit. It demanded only a business street and half a block cleared of parked cars on one side of the street. Christmas traffic made the downtown section out of the question. Moreover, while the California landscape at Christmas gives no hint of the season, the holly wreaths, Christmas trees and paper bells in every shop window gave more than a hint. We gave it up finally until after the holidays.

Gags, which are the lifeblood of comedies and which used to be our exclusive property, now are being conscripted into dramatic pictures regularly as comedy relief, not only in such war comedy dramas as *The Big Parade* and *What Price Glory?* but in so serious-minded a picture as *Sunrise*. The consternation of the young couple in the photographic studio in *Sunrise,* when they believe they have broken the Winged Victory or some such classically mutilated sculpture, was an old gag on the stage before the first picture was made.

Not only have the big producers notably increased the comedy content of their dramatic pictures in the last two or three years, but they have invaded directly our once private pasture with such new teams as Beery and Hatton, Bancroft and Conklin, Murray and Sidney, and Dane and Arthur, making straight comedies of program length. Charley Murray, George Sidney and Chester Conklin always have been comedians, but Beery, Hatton and Bancroft were menaces and character men who, cast in comedy-relief rôles, so stole the pictures from the dramatic leads that they were made stars and featured players on their comedy strength. Karl Dane and George Arthur jumped from obscurity to featured players on their comedy in one picture, *The Big Parade*. With the possible exception of straight love stories, there is an increasing emphasis everywhere on laughs. Among the women stars, Clara Bow, Bebe Daniels and Marion Davies now are *comédiennes* first and heroines only incidentally.

This new and earnest competition may have a pronounced effect upon what has been a separate branch of picture business; certainly we specialists in comedy never again will have the field so largely to ourselves. The long procession of love stories, Westerns, melodramas, costume romances and what not, lightened only by an occasional smile and depending largely on unrelated one-reel fillers for the laughs of the program, was poor showmanship, and I can't imagine a return to it.

Comedy demands a technic of its own, but the big producers have learned that. After attempting to make funny pictures with dramatic directors and failing, they have called in former comedy directors who had graduated to the larger field, of which there are many. Dramatic directors cannot time and space comedy, and actors accustomed only to dramatic work move too slowly through comedy scenes and fail to underscore their action properly.

One form of skill that all pictures demand alike is a knowledge of the limitations and values of a camera. It is all the audience a picture actor actually has. He is selling something to that black box on a tripod, and he must play the game by its rules; like the public, it is always right. Only what registers there reaches the screen. If he knows his camera well enough he can commit even the cardinal sin of pictures—to look directly into the lens. But he must know how to look into it without seeming to. And a secret of comedies, given away free with this volume, is that, if you make your audience hate your heavy sufficiently, you may heap the most outrageous slapstick upon him and have them cry for more.

On rainy days in the earliest period of the Roach company, we used to hug the fireplace in our room in the Bradbury house and try to read our futures in the eucalyptus embers. Roach had not yet sold a picture and his few thousands were melting fast, but he wore silk shirts.

"Do you suppose we ever will get anywhere?" he inquired one such day, as much of the fire as of the rest of the company. Which was as near pessimism as Hal permitted himself.

"Do you suppose this crazy business is going anywhere," some one else remarked, "or is it just another magic-lantern show?"

"Let's hear from Harold," Hal suggested. "What do you expect to be doing ten years hence? Or do you?"

Harold, who up to this time had taken no part in the conversation, replied, "I'll be pretty well satisfied if I can wear silk shirts like you." And Harold meant it. I was earning three dollars a day and paying fifteen dollars for suits at the Nebraska Clothiers.

Travel succeeded silk shirts as an ambition. It still is ungratified. I want more than ever to travel and am no nearer traveling, as I mean traveling. Once I was too busy earning a living, then too busy building a reputation, and now I am too busy holding a reputation, for Hollywood is no place to rest on one. Even the tortoises are fleet of foot out here, while the capacity of the public to forget a movie star is practically unlimited. Thus, having a reputation is not unlike having a bear by the tail. Any time I care to let go of the bear, I hear it suggested, I find any number of takers, but, alas, one grows fond of one's bear.

More than anything else, I would like to make a round-the-world tour, for I never have been out of North America. There are two obstacles. One is that it would be no fun unless the Lloyds could go just as another family of American tourists, and every one tells me that cannot be arranged. The other obstacle is the reason that keeps a Latin American dictator from running over to Paris any time he feels like it, or why congressmen go on kissing strange babies. They like the job and hope to keep it.

Any picture star is under certain obligations to what sometimes is known as "my public." Any picture star sounds a bit or more silly when he talks about "my public," but never think him or her hypocritical. That public is exactly as important as she or he pretends, which is as important as a parachute to a balloon jumper. To be a successful star in pictures, where audience and actor never meet and audiences are world-wide, demands even more trafficking in the actor's personality than the stage has set a precedent for. The whole purpose of publicity is to create a public interest in the actor, to make a public character of him. Having deliberately sought that interest, the actor cannot say: "You must excuse me; I am on public view only from three until five on alternate Wednesdays. The rest of my time I am a private citizen and I must ask you to respect my privacy." That is, he cannot say this if he goes abroad in public paths and if he hopes to keep his public.

There is good taste and bad taste in publicity, but, good and bad, Webster defines the word as "the quality of being public, or open to common knowledge." Wherefore, having solicited the public interest, I hardly could cross my fingers, cry Kings X and say I was not playing if the Lloyds made a world tour, yet who wants to circle the globe in a goldfish bowl?

There are celebrities—queens, politicians and actors—who frankly like the spotlight and are at their best under it. They give a good show. Why not? It is a much more logical and no less admirable attitude than that of the professional who strikes the modest pose. A Lindbergh has the right to accept or avoid public acclaim, as he chooses, but had he commercialized his name and fame he would have lost that amateur status.

It is no overpowering modesty that prevents me from showing myself in public *sans* make-up and out of character any more than I can help, so much as the fact that I do not give a good show. I never have got over being self-conscious and constrained on parade when out of make-up, and I do not look as I am supposed to look.

There is the further objection, I admit, that being on parade is stiff and itchy business and leaves no time for anything else. I feel like a boy with freshly washed ears and company manners, driven into the parlor to be introduced to Mr. and Mrs. Zwilch and little Millicent Zwilch. "Now run along, Harold, and show Millicent your magic lantern, and remember what I told you!"

We are returning by the southern route from one trip to New York. Eastward, we had gone by Canadian Pacific, and, going and coming, there had been receptions, appearances, welcoming speeches, parades and spontaneous outpourings of the populace, following on whispered hints from the publicity department. From Jacksonville to New Orleans—a long ride—nothing had been scheduled. Waking the next morning out of Jacksonville, I settled down to a day of solid comfort, which means whiskers and a lounging robe. The worse you look, the better you feel. There were sounds of a brass band when the train pulled into Mobile. I peered out, saw a crowd and a delegation on the platform, and was moved to glee.

"It's somebody else's turn," I chortled. "Don't cheer, boys; the poor devils are dying!"

Rap, rap, rap on the compartment floor. The New Orleans office enterprisingly had wired the Mobile office to scare up a demonstration for the visiting fireman. Unshaven and abashed, I had to go forth and grin foolishly at Mobile. With true Alabama courtesy, Mobile smiled back. Privately, however, I think they suspected, charitably, that I was not the true Harold Lloyd, but an impostor.

This suggests a story told in Hollywood on an independent producer of frugal methods. He was returning from a business trip to New York and his executives thought to honor and surprise the chief with one of those movie welcomes that sometimes land a photograph in the next day's papers. When the producer alighted this cloudless morning, he was greeted by his assembled company, flowers, music, camera clickings and huzzahs.

He fixed the assembled hired hands with a cold and rebuking eye. "What's this?" he asked, with rising inflection. "The sun is shining, ain't it?"

The Optic Theater, a ten-cent house on Main Street, Los

Angeles, was the scene of my first personal appearance. The theater showed the Lonesome Luke comedies regularly and the manager had wrung a promise from me to make a talk from his stage; I having a mental reservation that he would have to catch me first. Pollard and I attended the theater this night to see the first local showing of a blacksmith-shop comedy of the Luke series, and thought we were undetected.

In an intermission the manager stepped into the frame from which the illustrated songs were balladed, made his usual announcements and closed with the statement: "We have a nice surprise in store for you after the next picture."

Well, Snub and I liked surprises as well as the next one, and we waited with interest. When our comedy had been run, the manager appeared again. "I take great pleasure in announcing" —my startled ears heard—"that Mr. Harold Lloyd, whom you just have enjoyed as the inimitable Lonesome Luke, is in the audience. I am sure that he will be happy to come forward and say a few words to you. Mr. Lloyd, please."

The Optic was a converted storeroom with only one aisle down the center, and Pollard and I were trapped well toward the wall. Our only chance was that the manager did not know where we were sitting. We slid down in the seats and pulled our derbies down, but two ushers arrived shortly with requests to those on our left: "Would you mind standing up, please, to let Mr. Lloyd out?"

"What am I going to say?" I demanded of the manager when delivered into his hands.

"Oh, just any little thing," he said helpfully, and I found myself in the illustrated song frame. I had seen other butterflies racked on this wheel and knew some of the stock lines, such as: "We had a lot of fun making this picture and hope you may have had some in watching it," but I floundered painfully and suddenly blurted out: "Say, if any one in the audience knows what I am saying, he knows more than I do." The house liked that and laughed at everything I said thereafter. It might have been a triumph had I only known when and how to stop. I was too fussed to think of calling out Pollard, who was dying three deaths for fear I would denounce him to the mob.

Another night I did betray Pollard. He burst out of the theater but was caught and dragged back. Then I had to talk for him; he just stood grinning wryly. Dee Lampton, the fat boy of the earlier Luke comedies, also was in the audience, and to make the evening complete I called him out. Dee froze in his seat and might have escaped, but an old lady recognized him and with unconscious cruelty gave him over to the ushers. Fright paralyzed his vocal cords, which was the audience's loss, for he was a Southerner with a quaint combination of soft accents and high-pitched voice. Having him mute on my hands, I had to invent some nonsense about Dee being the champion pie eater of the Roach studio, with a record of fifteen in a day, and challenge the audience in his behalf to a contest.

Such experiences taught me not to put my trust in inspiration, but to memorize a few well-chosen words. Later Carter De Haven and I worked out a burlesque mind-reading act which served much better and which we used coöperatively. One sat on the stage blindfolded, the other passing along the aisles, borrowing objects from the audience and commanding his partner to identify them.

"What have I here?" the aisle man asks, holding up a stick pin. "Don't let this stick you."

"A stick pin!"—triumphantly from the stage.

"And this? Quick, let your answer ring clear and loud."

"A ring!"

"Watch out now! What is this I have borrowed from the gentleman in F-1?"

"I seem to see a watch."

"Sharp now! Can you see this one?"—with which the aisle man hums a bar from *Pagliacci* or *Carmen*.

"Is it, perhaps, a pair of opera glasses?"

Laying a hand upon a convenient bald head, the aisle man calls, "I have my hand upon an object. Use your head now. What is it?"

The correct answer from the stage is "Nothing," with which the aisle worker replies smartly, "Missed it by a hair."

Given a few lines or business, no actor will long be embarrassed in any theater. Take away his footlights, though, and he grows uneasy. In pictures it is location work and strangers on the studio set that test his poise. The bars have been raised high against visitors in the studios, not alone because they slow up work but for the further reason that casts frequently are nervous under the immediate tourist gaze. On location, where we work at the sufferance of the public, we are at their mercy. Los Angeles, fortunately, has grown blasé; the kids look on, but take it all in their stride.

Ending this detour and returning to ambitions; traveling for pleasure has been denied me, but money is a means to most ends eventually and, once my wages passed the margin of ordinary living expenses, money became an ambition. Not only money for its own sake, which I do not pretend to despise, but money as a measure of achievement.

About the time my salary jumped from $150 to $300 a week I set up that good old destination of $100,000 as a goal. One hundred thousand dollars used to be another way of saying independence. Invested in sound securities averaging 5 per cent, it returned an income of $5,000, a sum with which it seemed feasible to look the world in the eye and, if need be, tell it to go chase itself.

Success had been a long time on the road, but, when it did arrive, it came with such a cumulative rush that the $100,000 nest egg was laid before the nest was warm. The mark was set up to $500,000, then to $1,000,000. All out! End of the line! It was ridiculous to think of more. A great financier engaged in vast semipublic operations could use many millions to advantage, no doubt, but how could an ordinary citizen, putting his money to purely private uses, possibly need more than $50,000 a year income, backed up by $1,000,000 in the vault? I had the lesson of growing obligations yet to learn. We live on no steam-yacht or racing stable scale, yet an income of considerably more than $50,000 a year to-day requires no vast labor to manage nor ingenuity to get rid of, and, by the law of diminishing returns, it is no more exciting than the first silk shirt.

The first true luxury I ever allowed myself was a swimming pool at the Hoover Street home in my single days. To prevent the building of another house at too close quarters, we bought the vacant lot adjoining, and, having the additional grounds, built an outdoor pool and pergola at a cost of a few thousand dollars and had several times that much fun out of it. There is no swimming pool or other luxury about our present home; there will be, however, in our new place in Benedict Canyon, Beverly Hills.

We have been conservative in everything so far except this

new home, and we have tried, though with little success, to be conservative in this. I have the good judgment of my business manager, Mr. Fraser, to thank for owning the property—sixteen acres of the old Benedict ranch, including the home site. When he first suggested buying it, I laughed at him. It was fall, and fall in Southern California means dry streams and hills burned deep brown.

"What do I want with that gully and rock hillside?" I protested. "Besides, Beverly Hills is too far out."

Backed by the other officers of the company, Fraser persisted until I said, "All right! All right! But leave me out of it. Let it be a corporation deal purely and simply."

The corporation bought it and I did not go near it until the following spring. The stream was running, the arroyo and hills were green and flowering, and I began to perceive what landscaping and irrigation could do. We remodeled the old Benedict house and my mother occupied it for the next two years. During that time the influx into Beverly Hills set in; the first comer was the late Tom Ince, who built in the canyon just above us, a property now occupied by Carl Laemmle.

When Gloria was born, Mildred and I began to think seriously of building, but still we waited until assured that we could do it out of income rather than capital. After a year of consultation, planning and revising, we scrapped the first draft entirely. We wanted no formality. Our architect designed an Italian Renaissance house, formal and growing progressively more so.

In remodeling and redecorating my first house—the Hoover Street home—I had given an interior decorator his head, then hung, dragging on the reins, for a wild ride. This experience had left me a little gun-shy. Then a friendly architect dropped a hint. "Don't," he said, "build a monument to your architect; build a home for yourself." Unfortunately he failed to impart the secret of doing it.

This is a Golden Age for architects and landscape engineers in Southern California, a brave time, like the fifteenth century in the Italian cities. The conjunction of new wealth, enthusiasm, climate, irrigation and freedom of idea and expression is working magic in these hills. The Los Angeles district is one great experimental laboratory in which artists, draftsmen and engineers are working out a new and indigenous architecture, set in lovely scenes. They have the ideas, their customers have the

The Lloyds at play. The other man is *not* Paul Whiteman.

Harold and Mildred Davis Lloyd in the garden
of their Irving Boulevard home.

Harold playing handball.

Mrs. Lloyd on the tennis courts of their Beverly Hills home.

Gloria, the Lloyd heir, and her first birthday cake.

money, and the fur is flying—the fur being no dyed rabbit, but genuine customers' pelts.

After three years in the trenches, during which the Lloyds have conducted several strategic retirements, the war nears an end on our front. We are not quite sure who has won, but we know the casualties have been heavy. The landscaping is virtually completed and is a testimonial to the artistry and ingenuity of its designers. It would be a bold lad who would call our canyon a gully now. It supports a private nine-hole golf course, a canoe course, barbecue pavilion, a waterfall, forest paths, rocky glens, native and exotic plantings, a velvet turf and more, all of great charm and cunning. Such landscaping in the rainless months of California demands an elaborate irrigation system, with sprinklers set in the earth every few yards.

Another Italian Renaissance house, different in design from the first, is rising. It will not be mistaken for the Palace of Versailles or a moving-picture set, but it will be home. It stands on the site of the Benedict house, commanding a sweep of many miles southward to Los Angeles and west to the sea. Behind us a range—too high to be called hills, hardly high enough for mountains—is trellised with drives on which scattered new estates are trained, some of them as much as seven or eight hundred feet above us. Most of these homes are of that modified Mediterranean architecture which seems to blend best with the sunshine and the Pacific landscape, and most of them are the homes of picture people like ourselves.

An outdoor swimming pool, lounge, gymnasium and handball courts are taking shape. The tennis court is finished, also Gloria's own demesne—a thatched-roof old English cottage, pony stable and walled yard, all in minature and like an Edmund Dulac illustration for a story out of the Brothers Grimm.

Handball keeps me thin during the making of a picture, golf from getting too fat between pictures. I dare not look upon a midiron when a picture is making; golfers will know why without being told, and others could never understand, anyway. Douglas Fairbanks and I play often, and Mary finally chased me off the Pickfair private course the summer before last. I was free for a few days, but Douglas was presumed to be making *The Gaucho*. Handball is practicable because it may be played in the studio any idle hour.

Maynard Laswell, runner-up in 1923 and National A. A. U.

handball champion in 1924-25-26, used to be an extra at the Court Street studio and the first handball I ever saw was a game between Laswell and Roach at the Los Angeles Athletic Club. It is one of those deceptive sports which look so childishly simple to the spectator that he smiles indulgently. One day Roach jeered me onto the court by offering to spot me twenty points. Twenty-one is game.

"You mean that I have to make only one point to win?" I demanded.

"Right," said Roach, and won 21 to 0. I not only made no point, but rarely came within six inches of the ball. We started a second game. I made a wild swing at the ball, hit the side wall with my hand and sprained a thumb so that it was tied up for a week. Disgusted, I did not play again for years.

Some of us were killing time by batting a tennis ball against a building wall at the present studio one afternoon, and Jack Murphy, my production manager, was inspired to build a three-wall, open-air court, where we began playing regularly. Constant training and playing brought me to the point where I could make a respectable showing against Laswell on a three-wall court. Then the national-championship tournament was held at the Los Angeles Athletic Club on regulation four-wall indoor courts and Laswell won. He invited me to a return engagement on these courts and took three games with ridiculous ease. We were about to move our offices, necessitating tearing down the old court, so we built two new ones—one regulation, the other three-wall—both hidden inside a set purporting to be a cabaret. At first, when an opponent trimmed me on the standard court, I dared him over on the other for revenge, but now we play entirely on the four-wall court. The smack of the hard rubber ball on the wooden walls may be heard most any time of day at the Metropolitan studio, but, whether we find time to play during working hours or not, a set of handball concludes most every working day.

Sooner or later I shall be asked, "And to what do you attribute your success, Mr. Lloyd?" and I shall not blush and dimple and reply coyly that it is not for me to say. Nor shall I pretend to think that it was largely luck, for I do not think so, except in so far as all of life is a set of circumstances. The only ultimate answer would be "I attribute my success to being born," but the ingredients may be guessed at. The accident of growing up with a new theatrical form, enthusiasm, hard work and business sense have had much to do with it, but principally I have been an unusually successful picture comedian, I think, because I have an unusually large comedy vocabulary.

Vocabulary is not the right word, but I do not know a better. By it I mean the tools of my trade, the store of knowledge of comedy effects, what they are and how to obtain them, accumulated by long experience and observation, and sharpened by a natural instinct for the theater. The theater caught me young and no experience in it—cellar stage, amateur, stock company, stage hand, picture extra or one-reel slapstick—was wasted. Specialization plus aptitude plus work seems, therefore, after much figuring, to be the formula, which is no discovery. That answer was in the back of the book all along.

We have kept our pictures clean and will continue to do so. The easiest of laughs is the off-color gag. If it is well done and not too vulgar, adult audiences may enjoy it hugely yet not care to have their children see it, and we aim a picture at the whole family. Children are the easiest of audiences, business men the most difficult, and it is our particular pride that we draw both extremes as well as the middle.

How long I continue to make pictures will depend on how long I hold my popularity and avoid monotony in my stories. One, even two pictures, are no criterion, but if ever three fail consecutively the handwriting on the wall will need no translating. I can only hope that when the time comes I shall not try to fool either the public or myself, but will bow my way out as gracefully as I can manage and turn to directing, producing or developing a younger actor. I will not have the excuse others have had, if I do not. There are men and women in Hollywood who were so overwhelmed with sudden riches that they spent as they made. When their popularity waned they had no choice but to go on, good or bad.

If I keep the character genuine, however, and vary the theme sufficiently, I should continue in the comedy field indefinitely. The character is youth now. As my youth passes, either the character must grow older with me or I must switch to a new character.

In this year of 1928 the talking picture suddenly has become a fact. Yesterday it was a whisper, to-day it is a thunder clap, to-morrow it may bring revolution to Hollywood.

No one *can* predict and everyone *is* predicting what its effects will be. Apparently it will multiply many times the emotional appeal of the screen, opening unguessed possibilities. Apparently it will transform a technic that has been elaborated but has not changed since its birth. Apparently it will destroy old reputations at wholesale, make new ones, make the most lavish entertainment available to the smallest towns, throw thousands of theater orchestra musicians out of work, lead to the spending of several hundred millions of dollars in the next few years on studio and theater sound reproducing mechanisms, and act as a tremendous stimulus to the business. It may, moreover, move the royal capital from Hollywood back to New York City.

We are listening intently and moving cautiously. Our next picture will have a musical score and sound accompaniment; that we are agreed upon, and we are more than half persuaded to try dialogue. Meanwhile Hollywood is as jumpy as the second act of a mystery play, and elocutionists and other voice coaches are commanding bootleg prices in Beverly Hills. We shall see what we shall see and see it soon.

There are about 10,000 persons regularly employed in all capacities in the twenty-four studios in the Los Angeles district, fewer than half as actors. Some one has calculated that the odds against a girl becoming a star are 1 to 10,000, of becoming a featured player 1 to 2500, of appearing before the camera even as an extra, 1 to 100. Some one else has estimated that the odds against finding work of any sort in the studios, man or woman, are 1 to 450 and, incidentally, that the active career of a name in pictures averages less than five years.

Not a Chinaman's chance, in other words. Yet I would have my nerve, it seems to me, to advise any one to stay away. The odds were not so high in 1913, but were high enough. No one invited any of us to Hollywood; we came, we fought, we won. Our success will, with occasional exceptions, arrive by the same rocky road. The brief survival of the average picture name is as significant as the odds against the newcomer. It means, if the estimate is accurate, and I think it is approximately so, that 20 percent of the stars, directors and others at the top of the heap fall out of the race each year. Who takes their places? Well, not at any rate the boys and girls who were frightened off by the 1 to 10,000 odds.

For the first time in many years Hollywood was not confronted in 1927 with an acute problem of hordes of movie-struck girls, penniless and hopeless. Organized publicity finally has checked the flood and I would say no word to set it going again. Nevertheless, pictures demand youth as imperatively as athletics demand it, and youth will be served. The determined can not be kept away. They can only be warned to paste the odds in their hats, to bring money with them and to count the miles from Hattiesburg, for it is just as far going home.

They might remember that, while the stars get the publicity, they do not monopolize the money, nor all the interesting work in Hollywood. Directors, production managers, scenario editors, supporting players, title writers, supervisors and No. 1 cameramen earn from $150 to $7500 a week and contribute correspondingly to the success of the picture, though they may be obscured by the blinding light that beats upon the throne. There is a player in Hollywood who was starred thirty-five years ago in stage farces. He now plays regularly in the support of one picture star. His rôles are important to the picture, but relatively minor, and outside of the profession few know his name. Yet he gets $500 a week on a long-time contract in pictures, while at the height of his stage success his salary probably never was more than $200 a week.

They might remember, too, if they ever get as far as the extra list, that one way of getting farther is to study carefully the methods of their fellow extras, and do the opposite. More than half an extra's day is lost in tedious standing by, waiting on the director's call—tedious, that is, if the extra does not put it to some use. It might, for example, be translated into an education, specific or general. Privileged spectators, few bother to watch the action of the principals, their one opportunity of learning how. Few even listen to the director's instructions for their own work. Boredom would seem to suggest at least a book to read, but rarely does. Nor, I imagine, do the correspondence schools correct many Hollywood papers.

Hence when a boy and a girl of different stuff appear on the lot, the odds are not 1 to 10,000, nor 1 to 1,000. Most of the numbers against them are blanks. Janet Gaynor, one of the brightest prospects of the screen, was an extra not long ago. Charles Farrell, well up in the new crop of juvenile stars, worked extra for us in *The Freshman*. Most of the stars of to-morrow are unknowns of the extra list to-day, but they will not arrive by drowsing in the California sun, yarning and yawning and wondering why Janet Gaynor and Lon Chaney had all the luck.

APPENDIX

The Serious Business of Being Funny

an interview with Harold Lloyd

CONDUCTED AND EDITED BY HUBERT I. COHEN*

In November 1966, Harold Lloyd was promoting *The Funny Side of Life,* a second anthology made from his films. I [Hubert I. Cohen] was then the manager of the University of Michigan film society, The Cinema Guild, so I arranged to have Mr. Lloyd make a side trip to Ann Arbor to participate in a seminar at the University.

Mr. Lloyd's entrance was noteworthy. No sooner had this 73-year-old gentleman in a gray business suit entered the room than he sat down with his back toward us in a green-cushioned gray metal office chair on rollers that he found near the door. Planting his feet firmly on the floor, he pushed off, launching himself into the center of the room, where he came to a stop beside me and facing the audience. This kind of energy and enthusiasm characterized Mr. Lloyd throughout the interview.

I introduced Mr. Lloyd and conducted the interview. The following pages contain his answers to our questions at the meeting and to the questions I posed to him afterwards. (The questions are in italics.)

In the creation of a comic idea—when you went out to set up a scene—how did you know without an audience that a particular idea was going to be funny?

Lloyd: I'll answer that in a couple of different ways. Of

*This interview (Copyright © 1969 by Film Comment Publishing Corporation) originally appeared, in a somewhat different form, on pages 46 to 57 of Volume 5, Number 3 (Fall 1969 issue) of *Film Comment,* and is reprinted here by the kind permission of Austin F. Lamont, Managing Editor of *Film Comment,* and of Mr. Cohen.

course, you finally got to know by trial and error—you began to sense pretty well what was funny and what was not funny. But that's a long way from being a sure method. I was one of the first ones—I have been given credit for starting what they call "previews." Even back in the one-reel days, I would take a picture out to a theater when I knew the picture wasn't right. I wanted to get John and Mary's opinion of it. And the manager used to always have to come out and explain what was going on. When we were doing two-reelers, he came out in white tie and tails to do it and it was quite an event for him, and the audience would listen attentively. The audience didn't know what "previews" were, but there's nothing like an audience to tell you where you go wrong.

So that was one of the best methods we had and, I think, it saved us a great deal of—not that we didn't go off the track many times in spite of it—but it saved us many times because we would find out that certain sequences were splendid and others weren't. So we would come back in and go to work, and work for a month afterwards to remedy it, and if we found a scene wasn't as we wanted it, why, we would pull it out and try something else, then take it all out and "preview" it again. Of course, you can't always tell by that method, because all audiences are not the same.

You see, we all worked with what we called gag men, idea men, who helped us dig up an idea or to whom we'd give an idea to develop. We used to get together in what we called a gag room, and in these gag rooms I'd sit in with the boys for two or three hours a day, and they would all throw their ideas at me and it was up to me to choose from the ideas they came up with. Or else I'd have an idea and I'd say, "Here, let's work this around." Now, it was pretty hard ever to tell, in one of these sessions, whose the comedy idea was because from the time it was first brought in, it got so changed around, so twisted—or maybe it was a comedy idea that just needed embellishing. One of the things we did in those days was to get a good idea and then we did what we called "milking" it. We let it carry into many different types of humor. Now, I'll give you an example from *The Freshman* [1925]. We have a scene in there where the boy goes to a party with a basted suit. Well, now that's a funny idea in itself; it could be done in just one piece of business and then dismissed. But instead of that, we made a whole sequence out of it. It led from one thing to another, and inside of that one idea were more little complex ideas. When he had pulled a thread in his pants and his seams opened up, he had to have his pants sewed up, so in order to let the tailor sew it, he got into a very—and you'd have to see the picture to realize what he did—it looked like he was sitting down, but really from the waist down he was behind a curtain in back of him and back there the tailor was sewing his pants. And then other things happened—one gag led into the other.

I think that's the best way to let your humor come out, and it's one of the ways they don't do today. Very seldom do you see anyone taking advantage of the building of a gag, the pyramiding of it, where if it wasn't for the original piece of business you couldn't possibly do the second, and naturally not the fifth. That was one of the things that I think the comedians of our day did that they don't do today. Take Jerry Lewis, for example. He has a lot of talent, but his greatest failing, it seems to me, is that he doesn't build his gags this way.

How did you conceive and work out a purely visual gag like the one in The Funny Side of Life [*1966*] *in which it looks like you are sitting comfortably in the back seat of an open, moving car, whereas actually, when the car speeds away, we discover you are merely on a bike beside the car?*

LLOYD: Yes, now I remember that one; that happened to be my own personal gag. That's one of those illusion-type things. We had many of those that we all did. Sometimes it would look like you were on a ship and you were losing your cargo from the motion of the ship, if you get my point, and then you come up and you're not sick at all—maybe you've been down there fishing or something. This was that type of gag; they drop into that slot, and you try to get many variations of it. That was an exceptionally good illusion, because it *did* look exactly like I was sitting in the car, and, of course, I was riding a bicycle hanging onto the car, and, when we got ready, the car went on and I rode my bicycle up a driveway into the garage.

There are many different types. We had difficulty lots of times deciding whether we wanted the gag to be a surprise or whether we should let the audience in on it. You'd be surprised how important that is. Sometimes the surprise is much funnier, and sometimes when the audience realizes what's going to happen and anticipates it, it's more fun. So you really have to *judge*.

We had one piece of business that was always what we called "sure-fire"—a piece of comedy business that anybody can do and get big laughs. This particular one was down in the hold of a ship. This big fellow—we were having a fight—he was trying to kill me and nearing that objective. He threw me up against the side of this boat down in the hold and came over and picked up a big iron belaying-pin and took ahold of me and hit me over the head with this big iron—which should have crushed my skull. All I did was blink my eyes, and, of course, he was amazed and so naturally he struck me again, but with the same result. The third time he hit me, he even bent the bar. Then he was so flabbergasted he let go of me and as I chased away, you then see that when I was thrown against the wall, there was a bracket, an iron bracket, that fitted over my head. He was hitting the iron bracket, of course, and wasn't touching me at all, but you can't see that in the picture. That's a "sure-fire." Now, we did that two ways. We thought it would be good to let the audience know that the iron bracket was there. And the funny thing is, they laughed both ways. We had a hard time figuring which was better. We finally left it a surprise. I think surprise has a *sharper* laugh to it.

Generally, you can analyze why an audience doesn't laugh at a piece of business, but occasionally you can't. I had one failure that no one ever figured out. I was carrying a group of bundles —it was a marital story called *Hot Water* [1924]—and I was bringing home a turkey that I'd won in a raffle. I had taken my tie off and had tied it around the turkey's neck so I could lead it like a dog and carry my bundles at the same time. My shoe was untied so I set all of them down on one of these big mailboxes—you know, where you pile the mail packages on top—and as I sat down on the curb to tie my shoe, the postman came and picked up all my bundles with the mail, and I looked up just in time to see him starting to drive off with them. We always thought that was a very funny piece of business; it was a funny situation, but it *never* got a laugh. Oh, it got a titter, but not enough for the amount of footage we gave it. I never, to this day, have been able to figure out why that wasn't funny.

In *The Freshman,* we have a scene where I invite some of my fellow students to have an ice cream cone or soda or something, and they accept. Now, I invite only five or six, but as we go out, on our way to the ice cream parlor, they invite a few more and a few more and we finally end up with about fifty students going along. Well, we thought *that* was a *very* funny sequence. Originally, we really made a whole sequence of it. We went into the candy-soda fountain and, oh boy, we had some comedy business in there, very good gags *we* thought. But we didn't get laughs out of it. Finally, we analyzed it—the audience felt too sorry for the kid. They resented these students taking advantage of him the way they did. So not until we cut it out did the thing pull together.

Then you had to articulate and analyze the psychology of both the comic characterization and of the audience's response!

LLOYD: Oh, you had to—look, all the comedians of my day had to be *students* of comedy. You studied comedy, it just didn't happen, believe me.

Did you ever work from a fully developed script before you got into sound films?

LLOYD: I don't think we ever used a firm script till we did do a talking picture. In the real early days we really made them up as we went along—we picked a cast and went out to a park or some location and actually made up the picture. We did it in three or four days and that was about it. We'd make sequences chasing each other around trees or getting in a boat and we always had the heavy, and the comedian was always getting in trouble by picking somebody else's girl.

Of course, in the really early days, I was playing characters like Lonesome Luke and Willie Work, and they were grotesque-type characters with big shoes and funny moustaches and costumes—as I say, ludicrous. But even so, as we started making pictures with much more organized and with better type of material, we still didn't have an actual script. We had many *notes;* we had a pretty good outline of where we were going. We would work in our gag rooms, create our comedy ideas, and then we would go out with a pretty set idea of what we were going to shoot and what scenes we were going to do. But still, when we started shooting the scene, sometimes even though we'd shot the first scene maybe *exactly* as we wanted it, we would shoot it again, and maybe again and again, because we'd ad lib and do something entirely different. And, maybe, by the time we'd shot the scene seven times, we had changed it around so much that you wouldn't hardly know it from the first scene. And as I said before, sometimes we went back and took the first one if it was better than the others.

Did you find any problems in adjusting from the two-reeler to the bigger features?

LLOYD: From the two . . . we had a very natural changeover from the two-reeler. We started our first feature, really, *as* a two-reeler and it just grew up. It wasn't a feature; it was kind of a semi-feature. We called it *A Sailor-Made Man* [1921]. We started out for two reels but we seemed to have so much material that we were loath to stop, so Roach said, "Why the hell don't we just let it go and see where . . ." and it turned out to be a four-reeler. We thought, "Well, that film was more or less a matter of circumstance—it just happened that way," but the same thing happened with the next one. It was an idea that I'd had for a film for many years—we called it *Grandma's Boy* [1922]. I had tried to put the idea into a one-reeler years before and somehow we didn't do it, so we started it now as a two-reeler and *it* really kept growing and it somehow turned out to be our first feature-length picture. So it was a natural change-over—it wasn't one of these things "Now we'll do a longer type of picture."

We had almost the same transition from silent to sound. I had made this picture called *Welcome Danger* [1929] and I'd completed it in silent and we previewed it probably three or four times and had finally got it cut down to about where we thought it should be. (I found out afterwards it should still have had another reel cut out of it!) But I kept noticing that— now this is off the track, but you were talking about transitions —because sound was just coming in, little inconsequential things were getting tremendous laughs: like the frying of eggs—they'd howl at that. Or ice in a glass—it was funny to them. And then I said, "Here we're working our heads off, trying to get funny, humorous ideas, and we're getting them on these sound effects." I said, "Maybe we've kind of missed the boat; maybe we should make this film over." They were aghast at the idea, but I stuck to it and we did. We made half of it over and dubbed the other portion of it. The dubbing was terrible in those days. No one knew what they were doing, a large studio like that—we had everybody doing something different—it was like an insane asylum. We'd have one fellow walking up and down stairs [stamps his feet on the floor], another one rattling something here, another one there—if somebody'd come in, they'd have thought everybody'd lost their marbles. It's true! Of course, the dubbing today is entirely different.

But we managed a good transition from silent to sound because we already had the movement, the same type of action that we'd used in the silent picture, and then we added the sound to it.

It's claimed that some silent stars didn't make that transition from silence to sound because of their voices. Did you have a voice problem?

LLOYD: I had to work a little on my voice because I hadn't used it for years. I went to a voice coach for about . . . oh . . . five days, and then he said, "Goodbye, you just weren't using it right." I was talking [produces a falsetto] up here all the time. You know, you find a lot of girls—pardon me, girls, for doing this imitation—a lot of women don't use their voices right. They talk up here instead of doing it down here farther. But once he got me off on the right track, it was fine. But if you're working with somebody in the cast that has a stentorian voice, and you're talking up here, the microphone is going to have a hell of a time, I can assure you.

But, getting back . . . you were asking about using scripts. In a feature picture I like quite well—the one in which I'm hanging on the clock, *Safety Last* [1923], and which is probably one of our most popular—we did the final scenes of that climb *first*. We didn't know what we were going to have for the beginning of it. We hadn't made up the opening and after we found that we had, in our opinion, a very, very good thrill sequence, something that was going to be popular and bring in a few shekels, we went back and figured out what we would do for a beginning, and then worked on up to what we already had. Now, we tried the same thing in *The Freshman*. But there's a major difference. Now I'll bring up this point: I made two really different types of pictures. One was a *gag* type of picture where the picture depends mostly on the comedy business—*Safety Last* was such a picture. It had plenty of comedy ideas in it, and gags were salted all the way through—in a department store and finally on the side of the building. We had a gimmick that carried us into the climb because the character I was playing in that story *wasn't* supposed to be able to climb a building, but his pal, one of these steel workers on girders, was supposed to do it. But in the film, the pal gets into an altercation with this cop and *I* have to climb the building for him. Well, I *think* I will only have to climb to the first floor, but, of course, the cop finds out that my pal is in the building and begins chasing him around and from floor to floor and my pal keeps coming around to me and saying, "You gotta make it up just one more floor!" So we had that all the way up to the top, which as I say was the gimmick. . . . I'm telling it in a very cursory manner, but it still was one of the things that made our climb in *Safety Last* the best of all sequences, I think.

See, *Safety Last*—the *whole* picture was a gag type picture. *The Freshman,* on the other hand, is a character comedy. It starts much slower than a gag comedy. You have to condition it more, and it builds as it goes on. You have to plant your character and you get the audience completely with him; and you have to understand him and his background, and, definitely, his objective. The picture depends as much on the characterization and understanding of the boy as it does on the comedy business.

Did you prefer making "character" comedies over "gag" comedies?

LLOYD: I wouldn't say that. I think maybe my favorites are three that *are* character comedies. *Safety Last* is the only one of the four that I like the best that isn't a character comedy. The others are *Grandma's Boy, The Kid Brother* [1927] and *The Freshman*—and they are all character comedies. But I would say that the majority of the pictures that I made were gag comedies, *all* the two-reelers were gag comedies. I don't think we made a character comedy in two-reelers; they were all dependent on the gag business. In *The Freshman* we tried to shoot the football sequence—it's the best sequence, naturally—and we tried to do that sequence first just as we had the climb in *Safety Last*. We went out to the Rose Bowl, where we did a great deal of the picture, and we worked for about a week and a half, but it didn't come off, and it *didn't* come off because we didn't know the character at that time; we didn't understand him well enough, and we were off with the wrong kind of material. So we went back and did that story from the beginning, and the football game was shot *at the last.*

By the way, we were granted permission to do something that I don't think anyone was able to do at that time; we shot between halves during the California-Stanford game. They gave us permission, and in their card maneuvers on the side they had—of course, we couldn't use that in the picture—but, nevertheless, they had "Lloyd" spelled out and "Greetings" and "Welcome," too. We felt very much at home and we had a nice audience of about 90,000 to witness half a dozen of the scenes and we had to work pretty doggone fast there. Most of it *was* shot at the Rose Bowl game.

How would you characterize Chaplin's tramp and your boy with the glasses?

LLOYD: Well, Charlie generally had to play the losing lover because his character was the little tramp—who was a little grotesque. If he won the girl, she generally had to be off-beat, a little screwy. I had that grotesque quality when I did the characters *before* the boy with the glasses. But with this boy with the glasses character—that was one of his virtues, he wore ordinary clothes the same as the boy next door. He was somebody you'd pass on the street—and therefore his romances were believable. And I would say that I got the girl most every time. Generally, in many of Charlie's pictures, he walked down the road at the end, which had *its* own virtue.

It's a funny thing—they used to bracket Chaplin's pictures and mine in theaters, and until you see the two pictures run one after the other, not until then do you realize the entire difference between the way Chaplin worked and the way I worked. The difference didn't happen until after I had adopted the glasses. Before that, in the early days, I was more or less in the Chaplin bracket. He was completely the "King," and most everybody else was more or less an imitator of Charles. But when I adopted the glasses, I took on my own individuality and ceased to be in the same bracket.

You say you adopted the glasses as your trademark—what triggered this? A success in a particular film?

LLOYD: No, no. No, no. First, I was *looking* for a different character. A unique character is very difficult to establish. You see, in that period we all sought to have an identifying symbol or something. You had to have either a moustache, or a chin piece, or sideburns, or crossed eyes, or be fat or skinny or something that identified you. When they said "the fat man" or "the man with the funny moustache," or "the fellow with the little Dutch goatee" (that was Ford Sterling), or "the cross-eyed man" (that was Ben Turpin) —you had to have some kind of identifying characteristic. At least in those days we felt you did.

In a dramatic picture, I had seen a parson, a minister that wore glasses. They were hornrimmed glasses. He was a character that *appealed* to me. He was kind of a go-getter; he belied his appearance. You thought he was meek, mild, a placid type of character, but when he got riled up he was just the opposite. In fact, in one of the scenes a man was carrying off the girl and this meek-looking parson chased them on another horse and took the girl away and then jumped on the other horse and beat the other fellow up—really licked him—and when he got through, he just got up, casually dusted his clothes off and walked away. That character appealed to me. I was going to be doing a college series, and I thought that character was a good idea—"Why couldn't I do that?" At that time I was doing a picture called *Lonesome Luke* and Lonesome Luke was making a lot of money for the Hal Roach organization, and they thought I was out of my mind to want to change a character that was bringing in the money and that was fairly popular, too. I say it was more or less that I felt Luke was sort of an imitation of Chaplin— although I had tried to go the other way—I had *tight* clothes, etc., but nevertheless, Luke was in that category. So about a year later, I really had to tell them at Roach that I was leaving before they permitted me to try the character with the glasses. By that time, during that year, I'd lost the urge to make a college series and I just had the idea of a boy with glasses who didn't have to wear funny clothes. I could still use the same broad comic business, yet his romances would be believable. And so Roach turned me loose on my own. He then had a little clown character by the name of Toto who was a great favorite, one of the really great clowns of the world. Toto was playing at the Hippodrome in New York and Roach brought him out. The only problem was that Toto had a cast in his eye and was never really good material for films because of that. But Roach made many pictures with him—I guess he made, oh, six or seven or eight, but it didn't work. But my point is that Roach took over Toto and left me on my own. I had been making two-reel Lonesome Lukes, and they expected me to go on and make two-reel pictures with the glasses. But I made what I thought was a wise decision. I said, "No. I prefer to make one-reelers." And they thought I was out of my mind. "Why do you want to go back? Why do you want to retrogress when you've worked up to two-reelers? Why not carry on?" But I felt that you had to *introduce* the character; that *every* week you could come out with a one-reel picture and you could keep exposing your audience to this new character, whereas, with the two-reeler, you came out with only one every month. And this decision proved to be very valuable.

I had to think of all my own comedy business to start with, and I had to direct myself for about the first four films. Then I managed to get someone to work with me and direct it, a man by the name of Alf Goulding, who proved to be very good.

But when you say "starting out with a *character*"—this character of the boy with the glasses, you see, started off with an inner character that belied his outward appearance. He looked like he was a milk-and-toast character and anybody could push him around, but when you pushed him too far, he bounced back. So we had *that* to start with. And also, because he was not a grotesque, that character allowed us to do more *situation* than I had done before. But I never lost the idea of the gag or the carrying on. If you would look at my one-reelers and at my two-reelers, you would see a gradual transition.

You see, a lot of people get the idea that the pictures we made like *The Freshman* or *Safety Last* or *Grandma's Boy,* like Chaplin's *Gold Rush,* his *Limelight,* etc., were slapstick pictures. Well, that's really not true. There's a great deal of slapstick in 'em, but they are a blend of all the different types of comedy which we were able to develop. It was broad comedy, it was light comedy, it was farce comedy, there was a certain amount of dramatic comedy, but it is not true to say they are slapstick pictures just because there is a great deal of slapstick in the pictures. Now the one-reelers and a great many of the two-reelers were mostly slapstick, but as we got into the feature pictures that wasn't the case.

Did the personality of the boy with the glasses remain constant?

LLOYD: No. Whereas my character was always the boy with the glasses, and whereas he was always fighting odds, fighting the big fellows, still his attitude of thinking was entirely different from one character role to another—not that we didn't occasionally repeat the same type. Sometimes he was a brash character, sort of a go-getter like we have in *Safety Last;* another time, like in *Grandma's Boy,* he was a bashful, shy type of character. Sometimes he was rich, sometimes he was poor, sometimes he was a sophisticate, sometimes he was a dreamer, and each quality would motivate a lot of gags we'd do. Take the sophisticated character, for example. Do you remember the one I did in South America? What was the name of that one with the giant? . . . Yes, *Why Worry* [1923]. Now, that was a sophisticated type of character; he was sort of a hypochondriac, and your gags for that differed entirely—so did his thinking and his type of action—from the character in *Grandma's Boy.* So, in that way, my character was never just one straight-line character.

Originally, you directed and you were, of course, the chief performer. How would you evaluate your contribution as producer, director, and with regard to the creation of the comic ideas?

LLOYD: All right. That's a very good question. Practically all the top comedians had control of their pictures. Chaplin and I had almost complete control of our films. In my case, *after* a certain point Roach had control. But as time passed, Roach had other pictures and so I took over and I was completely responsible—even though Hal and I were partners. That's the reason we finally split up—it was his idea. He came to me and said, "Harold, I'm contributing . . . (this was near the time that we separated) . . . I'm contributing very little to your offers and I've got so many of my own, I think it's no more than fair that you should carry on on your own and have the whole thing." At that time, I was getting 75 percent of it and Hal was getting 25 percent. At first, I wasn't getting anything; I was being paid a salary. When I first went with him, I only got five dollars a day. I quit because he was giving somebody else ten and I wanted ten. I came back and he gave me $75.00 a week and that was a tremendous amount of money at that time; it was a big jump. But I would say that there wasn't a picture in which I wasn't in on the direction. Some of them I directed entirely on my own because most of the directors I had were boys who were gag men for me. I brought them in to direct a picture and made directors of them. Sam Taylor—who was one of the best I had and who afterwards went out and directed such individuals as John Barrymore, Mary Pickford, Douglas Fairbanks and Beatrice Lillie—well, he was a gag man and I brought him in to direct. He was probably the best I had. I never took credit, and I never have to this day, on the *direction* of a picture. On the production—producing it, yes. Even in pictures where I directed practically the whole thing, I didn't take the directing credit. In a talking picture called *Movie Crazy* [1932], I got one of the gag men to direct and he had a little difficulty with the bottle and we practically had to wash him out and I had to carry on. The writer in it I kept right at my elbow—a man by the name of Vincent Lawrence, a very fine playwright who had written many shows for Broadway—and I always had the advantage of his advice. *But* I still gave the credit to this other boy, the gag man, for it. I felt it helped them. I didn't see that it was going to add to my prestige, and certainly from a monetary standpoint it wasn't going to help me any more, and it did help them. The men who wanted to take credit for directing, they deserved it— they directed their pictures and had a perfect right to take the credit for it. I just didn't do it.

Would you describe what it was like working for Hal Roach and what kind of man he was?

LLOYD: Yes, I certainly would. I liked Hal very much. Hal and I kind of grew up together in the picture business. We were both extras together, and we both fought that business of whether we got three dollars or five dollars a day. He'd been in the theater for many years, done practically everything in the theater from call-boy in the burlesque shows to candy-butcher, usher, and practically everything else that you can think of that had to do with the theater.

Roach came into some money and asked me to go with him, and so we kind of grew up together in the motion picture end of it. Hal had a very excellent mind, a very fertile mind for thinking of comedy ideas. But because he hadn't had the experience, he wasn't quite as good at setting up a scene. There were many times, even in the very early days, Hal would say, "How would you do *this*, Harold?" Now, he was the boss and it was his company and I was working for him. Sometimes we'd be working on a beach where we maybe had two or three hundred people watching us, and Hal, in those early days, would be a little embarrassed because he didn't know just how to set it up. So I more or less took over and helped him. But we were able to work hand and glove, and figure out ideas together, and it was wonderful . . . it was a wonderful relationship. We'd get mad at each other once in a while, but we'd always make up. We had a little altercation not so long ago—he thought that I had done something I didn't, but when we met in New York about four months ago, it was all brushed aside again just as before. I would say that for that time and type of picture, Hal was one of the really pioneer, fine, comedy producers like Mack Sennett.

Some of the scenes in your pictures are pretty hair-raising— the chase sequences, for example. Do you recall anything that happened accidentally during the shooting that you then worked into your film?

LLOYD: Oh, yes, many, many times. One we had . . . I don't know how many of you saw the picture called *World of Comedy* [1962; the first anthology made from some of Lloyd's films, edited by Lloyd] that I did not so long ago. In it we had a chase, a very good chase I thought, one of the best that I ever made—from *Girl Shy* [1924]. In this sequence, I was getting on many different vehicles; I was trying to save my girl from being married to a terrible villain that was already married. I was on this horse and the horse wasn't expected to fall. Yet in this picture you'll see that it does fall. He's running at head speed and slips and falls. Well, that was not supposed to be that way. We cut to the close-up and afterwards the horse got up and away we went again. That was kept in.

Another time, we were doing a picture where these horses we were driving—we actually did that in New York, driving right down Broadway . . . oh, we'd go for about three blocks—we had our own policemen, our own traffic cars and so forth and . . . Oh, I remember one shot we were never able to keep in—one of our cars got in the way of one of our horses as it was racing down Broadway and the horse went down the subway! Fortunately for us the horse was all right. He wasn't hurt; he was a little [pause] shaken up. We weren't able to use him any more!

One shot we did use—we were going down Third Avenue when

it still had the El. We were taking this heavy streetcar down Third Avenue when—bing! we crashed into one of the El posts. I didn't happen to be driving—that was one of the few things that I wasn't able to do. We had a rodeo driver. I would have killed the horses and everyone else trying to do that; I wasn't a good enough driver to do that. But this streetcar hit and away this driver flew, head first right out, and lit on his face. Well, we kept that in.

So, we've had a number of things that happened like that. Sometimes in balancing on ledges in some of those thrill pictures we did, sometimes I would push it a little extra far. And it was a good thing that we had a platform built below me, because when I found that I had gone a little too far, it enabled me to jump down to it—because we were actually up as high as you see me in the picture. If it shows nine or ten stories in the air, that's where it was. Passers-by were there at the time—they didn't know we were shooting, of course, they weren't supposed to be looking at us. But, anyhow, sometimes you wouldn't think and you'd take a chance and you'd go very far out. Oh, there were many times. . . . I know one time that I caught on the back end of a fire engine and it had this hose and the business was, the gag was, that the hose was loose and as I grabbed ahold of the nozzle the hose started to unwind and I began pulling it like that [begins to act it out] and, of course, I began to lose out in the struggle and finally I was practically parallel with the street still hanging onto this hose, which was supposed to be fastened on at the end and holding me. But something went askew, and it came off and hit me in the head with the big brass nozzle, and off I went. I was out for about five minutes. Somebody asked me if I was all right and I said, "Well, I could have got along without that!" We didn't keep that shot in. You can't show people *really* getting injured—audiences just won't laugh.

What role did musical accompaniment play in your silent films?

LLOYD: Many people don't realize this today, but you have to have music with silent films. We never ran them without music. Music creates a tremendous atmosphere, a mood. It is an amazing thing. The music just lifts a picture up—it really does something for it.

In museums, there is often an erroneous presentation of silent films. They take feature films and play them with a lone piano accompaniment. We *never* showed them that way. It is entirely wrong. We either had a full orchestra and showed them twice a day, or the films were accompanied by a large pipe organ—either a Wurlitzer or a Kimball. But at no time, unless it was in some small village where they couldn't afford it, did they play it on the piano. Never in the city or in a large place.

And we used to give out a musical score with our pictures. And I'd say that about two-thirds of the time the orchestra leader never followed these scores, but gave out his own. In addition, we always had a hassle with them about when to play loudly or quietly. When the picture wasn't getting any laughs, they'd play *very* pianissimo, but the moment the laughs started to come, up they came with the music and then you couldn't hear the laughs.

Would you comment on Chaplin's exile and his art?

LLOYD: Well, I think he should return to the United States. After all, I don't think that they should allow his talents as a great comedian to interfere . . . although he did transgress quite a bit, I think, in some of his action. Some of the women's clubs, I understand, were more or less responsible for taking action against Charles. But I think it's high time that he did come back.

He's a tremendous personality in the theater, one of the greatest. Chaplin . . . I'd put him down as the finest pantomimist that I know: he is the greatest in pantomime. We've had some very fine ones. I think we have a very good one that's been in television for a long time—Red Skelton, but his pantomime is different. The same . . . what is the other fellow's name—oh yes, Marcel Marceau. He's a very fine pantomimist, but entirely different. Skelton's, Chaplin's and Marceau's pantomime are entirely different. Of course, in the early days of the film we all had to know pantomime. We had to get away from that "I," "you," and the old crude stuff which they did way, way back. You had to have pantomime down so well that you didn't realize that you were doing pantomime. The funny thing is that in pictures without the voice, if you have a good picture, people soon forget that you're not talking and don't seem to give a damn. That's if your picture is good enough. If your picture isn't good [he laughs aloud], you probably wish that you were talking.

Index

Only names of persons and titles of films and plays are included. The names of characters created by Harold Lloyd appear in quotation marks. Unnumbered illustration pages are listed as 8A (page following page 8), 8B (the page after that), etc.

A CATALOGUE OF SELECTED DOVER BOOKS
IN ALL FIELDS OF INTEREST

A CATALOGUE OF SELECTED DOVER BOOKS
IN ALL FIELDS OF INTEREST

AMERICA'S OLD MASTERS, James T. Flexner. Four men emerged unexpectedly from provincial 18th century America to leadership in European art: Benjamin West, J. S. Copley, C. R. Peale, Gilbert Stuart. Brilliant coverage of lives and contributions. Revised, 1967 edition. 69 plates. 365pp. of text.

21806-6 Paperbound $3.00

FIRST FLOWERS OF OUR WILDERNESS: AMERICAN PAINTING, THE COLONIAL PERIOD, James T. Flexner. Painters, and regional painting traditions from earliest Colonial times up to the emergence of Copley, West and Peale Sr., Foster, Gustavus Hesselius, Feke, John Smibert and many anonymous painters in the primitive manner. Engaging presentation, with 162 illustrations. xxii + 368pp.

22180-6 Paperbound $3.50

THE LIGHT OF DISTANT SKIES: AMERICAN PAINTING, 1760-1835, James T. Flexner. The great generation of early American painters goes to Europe to learn and to teach: West, Copley, Gilbert Stuart and others. Allston, Trumbull, Morse; also contemporary American painters—primitives, derivatives, academics—who remained in America. 102 illustrations. xiii + 306pp.

22179-2 Paperbound $3.00

A HISTORY OF THE RISE AND PROGRESS OF THE ARTS OF DESIGN IN THE UNITED STATES, William Dunlap. Much the richest mine of information on early American painters, sculptors, architects, engravers, miniaturists, etc. The only source of information for scores of artists, the major primary source for many others. Unabridged reprint of rare original 1834 edition, with new introduction by James T. Flexner, and 394 new illustrations. Edited by Rita Weiss. 6⅝ x 9⅝.

21695-0, 21696-9, 21697-7 Three volumes, Paperbound $13.50

EPOCHS OF CHINESE AND JAPANESE ART, Ernest F. Fenollosa. From primitive Chinese art to the 20th century, thorough history, explanation of every important art period and form, including Japanese woodcuts; main stress on China and Japan, but Tibet, Korea also included. Still unexcelled for its detailed, rich coverage of cultural background, aesthetic elements, diffusion studies, particularly of the historical period. 2nd, 1913 edition. 242 illustrations. lii + 439pp. of text.

20364-6, 20365-4 Two volumes, Paperbound $6.00

THE GENTLE ART OF MAKING ENEMIES, James A. M. Whistler. Greatest wit of his day deflates Oscar Wilde, Ruskin, Swinburne; strikes back at inane critics, exhibitions, art journalism; aesthetics of impressionist revolution in most striking form. Highly readable classic by great painter. Reproduction of edition designed by Whistler. Introduction by Alfred Werner. xxxvi + 334pp.

21875-9 Paperbound $2.50

A HISTORY OF COSTUME, Carl Köhler. Definitive history, based on surviving pieces of clothing primarily, and paintings, statues, etc. secondarily. Highly readable text, supplemented by 594 illustrations of costumes of the ancient Mediterranean peoples, Greece and Rome, the Teutonic prehistoric period; costumes of the Middle Ages, Renaissance, Baroque, 18th and 19th centuries. Clear, measured patterns are provided for many clothing articles. Approach is practical throughout. Enlarged by Emma von Sichart. 464pp. 21030-8 Paperbound $3.50

ORIENTAL RUGS, ANTIQUE AND MODERN, Walter A. Hawley. A complete and authoritative treatise on the Oriental rug—where they are made, by whom and how, designs and symbols, characteristics in detail of the six major groups, how to distinguish them and how to buy them. Detailed technical data is provided on periods, weaves, warps, wefts, textures, sides, ends and knots, although no technical background is required for an understanding. 11 color plates, 80 halftones, 4 maps. vi + 320pp. 6⅛ x 9⅛. 22366-3 Paperbound $5.00

TEN BOOKS ON ARCHITECTURE, Vitruvius. By any standards the most important book on architecture ever written. Early Roman discussion of aesthetics of building, construction methods, orders, sites, and every other aspect of architecture has inspired, instructed architecture for about 2,000 years. Stands behind Palladio, Michelangelo, Bramante, Wren, countless others. Definitive Morris H. Morgan translation. 68 illustrations. xii + 331pp. 20645-9 Paperbound $3.50

THE FOUR BOOKS OF ARCHITECTURE, Andrea Palladio. Translated into every major Western European language in the two centuries following its publication in 1570, this has been one of the most influential books in the history of architecture. Complete reprint of the 1738 Isaac Ware edition. New introduction by Adolf Placzek, Columbia Univ. 216 plates. xxii + 110pp. of text. 9½ x 12¾. 21308-0 Clothbound $10.00

STICKS AND STONES: A STUDY OF AMERICAN ARCHITECTURE AND CIVILIZATION, Lewis Mumford.One of the great classics of American cultural history. American architecture from the medieval-inspired earliest forms to the early 20th century; evolution of structure and style, and reciprocal influences on environment. 21 photographic illustrations. 238pp. 20202-X Paperbound $2.00

THE AMERICAN BUILDER'S COMPANION, Asher Benjamin. The most widely used early 19th century architectural style and source book, for colonial up into Greek Revival periods. Extensive development of geometry of carpentering, construction of sashes, frames, doors, stairs; plans and elevations of domestic and other buildings. Hundreds of thousands of houses were built according to this book, now invaluable to historians, architects, restorers, etc. 1827 edition. 59 plates. 114pp. 7⅞ x 10¾. 22236-5 Paperbound $3.50

DUTCH HOUSES IN THE HUDSON VALLEY BEFORE 1776, Helen Wilkinson Reynolds. The standard survey of the Dutch colonial house and outbuildings, with constructional features, decoration, and local history associated with individual homesteads. Introduction by Franklin D. Roosevelt. Map. 150 illustrations. 469pp. 6⅝ x 9¼. 21469-9 Paperbound $4.00

THE ARCHITECTURE OF COUNTRY HOUSES, Andrew J. Downing. Together with Vaux's *Villas and Cottages* this is the basic book for Hudson River Gothic architecture of the middle Victorian period. Full, sound discussions of general aspects of housing, architecture, style, decoration, furnishing, together with scores of detailed house plans, illustrations of specific buildings, accompanied by full text. Perhaps the most influential single American architectural book. 1850 edition. Introduction by J. Stewart Johnson. 321 figures, 34 architectural designs. xvi + 560pp.
22003-6 Paperbound $4.00

LOST EXAMPLES OF COLONIAL ARCHITECTURE, John Mead Howells. Full-page photographs of buildings that have disappeared or been so altered as to be denatured, including many designed by major early American architects. 245 plates. xvii + 248pp. 7⅞ x 10¾. 21143-6 Paperbound $3.50

DOMESTIC ARCHITECTURE OF THE AMERICAN COLONIES AND OF THE EARLY REPUBLIC, Fiske Kimball. Foremost architect and restorer of Williamsburg and Monticello covers nearly 200 homes between 1620-1825. Architectural details, construction, style features, special fixtures, floor plans, etc. Generally considered finest work in its area. 219 illustrations of houses, doorways, windows, capital mantels. xx + 314pp. 7⅞ x 10¾. 21743-4 Paperbound $4.00

EARLY AMERICAN ROOMS: 1650-1858, edited by Russell Hawes Kettell. Tour of 12 rooms, each representative of a different era in American history and each furnished, decorated, designed and occupied in the style of the era. 72 plans and elevations, 8-page color section, etc., show fabrics, wall papers, arrangements, etc. Full descriptive text. xvii + 200pp. of text. 8⅜ x 11¼.
21633-0 Paperbound $5.00

THE FITZWILLIAM VIRGINAL BOOK, edited by J. Fuller Maitland and W. B. Squire. Full modern printing of famous early 17th-century ms. volume of 300 works by Morley, Byrd, Bull, Gibbons, etc. For piano or other modern keyboard instrument; easy to read format. xxxvi + 938pp. 8⅜ x 11.
21068-5, 21069-3 Two volumes, Paperbound $10.00

KEYBOARD MUSIC, Johann Sebastian Bach. Bach Gesellschaft edition. A rich selection of Bach's masterpieces for the harpsichord: the six English Suites, six French Suites, the six Partitas (Clavierübung part I), the Goldberg Variations (Clavierübung part IV), the fifteen Two-Part Inventions and the fifteen Three-Part Sinfonias. Clearly reproduced on large sheets with ample margins; eminently playable. vi + 312pp. 8⅛ x 11. 22360-4 Paperbound $5.00

THE MUSIC OF BACH: AN INTRODUCTION, Charles Sanford Terry. A fine, nontechnical introduction to Bach's music, both instrumental and vocal. Covers organ music, chamber music, passion music, other types. Analyzes themes, developments, innovations. x + 114pp. 21075-8 Paperbound $1.25

BEETHOVEN AND HIS NINE SYMPHONIES, Sir George Grove. Noted British musicologist provides best history, analysis, commentary on symphonies. Very thorough, rigorously accurate; necessary to both advanced student and amateur music lover. 436 musical passages. vii + 407 pp. 20334-4 Paperbound $2.75

POEMS OF ANNE BRADSTREET, edited with an introduction by Robert Hutchinson. A new selection of poems by America's first poet and perhaps the first significant woman poet in the English language. 48 poems display her development in works of considerable variety—love poems, domestic poems, religious meditations, formal elegies, "quaternions," etc. Notes, bibliography. viii + 222pp.

22160-1 Paperbound $2.00

THREE GOTHIC NOVELS: THE CASTLE OF OTRANTO BY HORACE WALPOLE; VATHEK BY WILLIAM BECKFORD; THE VAMPYRE BY JOHN POLIDORI, WITH FRAGMENT OF A NOVEL BY LORD BYRON, edited by E. F. Bleiler. The first Gothic novel, by Walpole; the finest Oriental tale in English, by Beckford; powerful Romantic supernatural story in versions by Polidori and Byron. All extremely important in history of literature; all still exciting, packed with supernatural thrills, ghosts, haunted castles, magic, etc. xl + 291pp.

21232-7 Paperbound $2.50

THE BEST TALES OF HOFFMANN, E. T. A. Hoffmann. 10 of Hoffmann's most important stories, in modern re-editings of standard translations: Nutcracker and the King of Mice, Signor Formica, Automata, The Sandman, Rath Krespel, The Golden Flowerpot, Master Martin the Cooper, The Mines of Falun, The King's Betrothed, A New Year's Eve Adventure. 7 illustrations by Hoffmann. Edited by E. F. Bleiler. xxxix + 419pp.

21793-0 Paperbound $3.00

GHOST AND HORROR STORIES OF AMBROSE BIERCE, Ambrose Bierce. 23 strikingly modern stories of the horrors latent in the human mind: The Eyes of the Panther, The Damned Thing, An Occurrence at Owl Creek Bridge, An Inhabitant of Carcosa, etc., plus the dream-essay, Visions of the Night. Edited by E. F. Bleiler. xxii + 199pp.

20767-6 Paperbound $1.50

BEST GHOST STORIES OF J. S. LeFANU, J. Sheridan LeFanu. Finest stories by Victorian master often considered greatest supernatural writer of all. Carmilla, Green Tea, The Haunted Baronet, The Familiar, and 12 others. Most never before available in the U. S. A. Edited by E. F. Bleiler. 8 illustrations from Victorian publications. xvii + 467pp.

20415-4 Paperbound $3.00

MATHEMATICAL FOUNDATIONS OF INFORMATION THEORY, A. I. Khinchin. Comprehensive introduction to work of Shannon, McMillan, Feinstein and Khinchin, placing these investigations on a rigorous mathematical basis. Covers entropy concept in probability theory, uniqueness theorem, Shannon's inequality, ergodic sources, the E property, martingale concept, noise, Feinstein's fundamental lemma, Shanon's first and second theorems. Translated by R. A. Silverman and M. D. Friedman. iii + 120pp.

60434-9 Paperbound $1.75

SEVEN SCIENCE FICTION NOVELS, H. G. Wells. The standard collection of the great novels. Complete, unabridged. *First Men in the Moon, Island of Dr. Moreau, War of the Worlds, Food of the Gods, Invisible Man, Time Machine, In the Days of the Comet.* Not only science fiction fans, but every educated person owes it to himself to read these novels. 1015pp.

20264-X Clothbound $5.00

HOW TO KNOW THE WILD FLOWERS, Mrs. William Starr Dana. This is the classical book of American wildflowers (of the Eastern and Central United States), used by hundreds of thousands. Covers over 500 species, arranged in extremely easy to use color and season groups. Full descriptions, much plant lore. This Dover edition is the fullest ever compiled, with tables of nomenclature changes. 174 full-page plates by M. Satterlee. xii + 418pp.   20332-8 Paperbound $2.75

OUR PLANT FRIENDS AND FOES, William Atherton DuPuy. History, economic importance, essential botanical information and peculiarities of 25 common forms of plant life are provided in this book in an entertaining and charming style. Covers food plants (potatoes, apples, beans, wheat, almonds, bananas, etc.), flowers (lily, tulip, etc.), trees (pine, oak, elm, etc.), weeds, poisonous mushrooms and vines, gourds, citrus fruits, cotton, the cactus family, and much more. 108 illustrations. xiv + 290pp.   22272-1 Paperbound $2.50

HOW TO KNOW THE FERNS, Frances T. Parsons. Classic survey of Eastern and Central ferns, arranged according to clear, simple identification key. Excellent introduction to greatly neglected nature area. 57 illustrations and 42 plates. xvi + 215pp.   20740-4 Paperbound $2.00

MANUAL OF THE TREES OF NORTH AMERICA, Charles S. Sargent. America's foremost dendrologist provides the definitive coverage of North American trees and tree-like shrubs. 717 species fully described and illustrated: exact distribution, down to township; full botanical description; economic importance; description of subspecies and races; habitat, growth data; similar material. Necessary to every serious student of tree-life. Nomenclature revised to present. Over 100 locating keys. 783 illustrations. lii + 934pp. 20277-1, 20278-X Two volumes, Paperbound $6.00

OUR NORTHERN SHRUBS, Harriet L. Keeler. Fine non-technical reference work identifying more than 225 important shrubs of Eastern and Central United States and Canada. Full text covering botanical description, habitat, plant lore, is paralleled with 205 full-page photographs of flowering or fruiting plants. Nomenclature revised by Edward G. Voss. One of few works concerned with shrubs. 205 plates, 35 drawings. xxviii + 521pp.   21989-5 Paperbound $3.75

THE MUSHROOM HANDBOOK, Louis C. C. Krieger. Still the best popular handbook: full descriptions of 259 species, cross references to another 200. Extremely thorough text enables you to identify, know all about any mushroom you are likely to meet in eastern and central U. S. A.: habitat, luminescence, poisonous qualities, use, folklore, etc. 32 color plates show over 50 mushrooms, also 126 other illustrations. Finding keys. vii + 560pp.   21861-9 Paperbound $3.95

HANDBOOK OF BIRDS OF EASTERN NORTH AMERICA, Frank M. Chapman. Still much the best single-volume guide to the birds of Eastern and Central United States. Very full coverage of 675 species, with descriptions, life habits, distribution, similar data. All descriptions keyed to two-page color chart. With this single volume the average birdwatcher needs no other books. 1931 revised edition. 195 illustrations. xxxvi + 581pp.   21489-3 Paperbound $4.50

MATHEMATICAL PUZZLES FOR BEGINNERS AND ENTHUSIASTS, Geoffrey Mott-Smith. 189 puzzles from easy to difficult—involving arithmetic, logic, algebra, properties of digits, probability, etc.—for enjoyment and mental stimulus. Explanation of mathematical principles behind the puzzles. 135 illustrations. viii + 248pp.
20198-8 Paperbound $1.75

PAPER FOLDING FOR BEGINNERS, William D. Murray and Francis J. Rigney. Easiest book on the market, clearest instructions on making interesting, beautiful origami. Sail boats, cups, roosters, frogs that move legs, bonbon boxes, standing birds, etc. 40 projects; more than 275 diagrams and photographs. 94pp.
20713-7 Paperbound $1.00

TRICKS AND GAMES ON THE POOL TABLE, Fred Herrmann. 79 tricks and games— some solitaires, some for two or more players, some competitive games—to entertain you between formal games. Mystifying shots and throws, unusual caroms, tricks involving such props as cork, coins, a hat, etc. Formerly *Fun on the Pool Table.* 77 figures. 95pp.
21814-7 Paperbound $1.00

HAND SHADOWS TO BE THROWN UPON THE WALL: A SERIES OF NOVEL AND AMUSING FIGURES FORMED BY THE HAND, Henry Bursill. Delightful picturebook from great-grandfather's day shows how to make 18 different hand shadows: a bird that flies, duck that quacks, dog that wags his tail, camel, goose, deer, boy, turtle, etc. Only book of its sort. vi + 33pp. 6½ x 9¼. 21779-5 Paperbound $1.00

WHITTLING AND WOODCARVING, E. J. Tangerman. 18th printing of best book on market. "If you can cut a potato you can carve" toys and puzzles, chains, chessmen, caricatures, masks, frames, woodcut blocks, surface patterns, much more. Information on tools, woods, techniques. Also goes into serious wood sculpture from Middle Ages to present, East and West. 464 photos, figures. x + 293pp.
20965-2 Paperbound $2.00

HISTORY OF PHILOSOPHY, Julián Marias. Possibly the clearest, most easily followed, best planned, most useful one-volume history of philosophy on the market; neither skimpy nor overfull. Full details on system of every major philosopher and dozens of less important thinkers from pre-Socratics up to Existentialism and later. Strong on many European figures usually omitted. Has gone through dozens of editions in Europe. 1966 edition, translated by Stanley Appelbaum and Clarence Strowbridge. xviii + 505pp. 21739-6 Paperbound $3.00

YOGA: A SCIENTIFIC EVALUATION, Kovoor T. Behanan. Scientific but non-technical study of physiological results of yoga exercises; done under auspices of Yale U. Relations to Indian thought, to psychoanalysis, etc. 16 photos. xxiii + 270pp.
20505-3 Paperbound $2.50

Prices subject to change without notice.
Available at your book dealer or write for free catalogue to Dept. GI, Dover Publications, Inc., 180 Varick St., N. Y., N. Y. 10014. Dover publishes more than 150 books each year on science, elementary and advanced mathematics, biology, music, art, literary history, social sciences and other areas.